"Ich Kuss die Hand"

Edited by

Peter W. Dowell

"Ich Kuss die Hand"

The Letters of

H. L. Mencken

to Gretchen Hood

The University of

Alabama Press

Copyright © 1986 by

The University of Alabama Press

University, Alabama 35486

All rights reserved

Manufactured in the

United States of America

Library of Congress Cataloging-in-Publication Data

Mencken, H. L. (Henry Louis), 1880–1956.

"Ich kuss die Hand".

   Includes index.
      1. Mencken, H. L. (Henry Louis), 1880–1956—
Correspondence.   2. Authors, American—20th
century—Correspondence.   3. Hood, Gretchen—
Correspondence.   I. Hood, Gretchen.   II. Dowell,
Peter W., 1937–   .   III. Title.
PS3525.E43Z485   1986   818'.5209 [B]   85–20987
ISBN 0–8173–0296–4 (alk. paper)

Contents

Acknowledgments

The completion of this book owes much to the various kinds of aid I received from several sources. Linda Matthews, Virginia Cain, Holly Crenshaw, and Diane Windham provided assistance and cheerful encouragement that made it a genuine pleasure to work with the Mencken/ Hood Collection in the Special Collections Department of the Woodruff Library at Emory University. Marie and Eric Nitschke of the library's Reference Department helped me on several occasions to track down needed information. Barbara Vandergrift, Archivist for the National Press Club, gave me access to its materials on Gretchen Hood. I also appreciate the efforts by John Emerson of the Music Library at the University of California, Berkeley, to unearth information about Hood's operatic career. Helen Fontsere contributed greatly to the preparation of the manuscript, and Trudy Kretchman aided me in too many ways to enumerate. My research was facilitated by being able to work in the Manuscripts and the Newspaper Divisions of the New York Public Library and the Washingtoniana Division of the Martin Luther King Memorial Library in Washington, D.C.

The Enoch Pratt Free Library of Baltimore, in accordance with the terms of the will of H. L. Mencken, has granted me permission to print the texts of his letters to Hood. Permission to quote her notes to the letters and copies of her extant letters to Mencken comes from the Trust Officers' Committee of the NS&T Bank of Washington, D.C., as the administrators of her estate; from the Robert W. Woodruff Library; and from the Julia Rogers Library of Goucher College.

I am indebted to the Emory University Research Committee for a grant in support of the project.

I wish especially to express my appreciation to May M. Dowell for her assistance in discovering materials pertaining to Gretchen Hood at the New York Public Library, the New-York Historical Society, and the Library of the Performing Arts at Lincoln Center; to my colleague William B. Dillingham for his careful reading of the introduction and his continual good counsel as the work progressed; and finally to Valerie and Jonathan, for whose patience and understanding I am more grateful than they know.

"Ich Kuss die Hand"

Introduction

In December 1926, when he first wrote Gretchen Hood, H. L. Mencken was at the peak of his reputation and influence as a trenchant satirical commentator on contemporary American life. Now about to enter its fourth year, the *American Mercury,* bearing his indelible editorial stamp in all its features, had established itself as one of the country's most popular intellectual journals. His *Notes on Democracy* and the fifth series of *Prejudices* had recently been published, and he aired his views as well through his Monday articles on the editorial pages of the *Baltimore Evening Sun* and a syndicated column for the *Chicago Sunday Tribune.* Seventeen months earlier, he had gained nationwide attention when he pilloried William Jennings Bryan and the Fundamentalist opponents of teaching evolution at the Scopes Trial in Dayton, Tennessee. He had made headlines in April 1926 by defying the local censors and getting himself arrested on the Boston Common for selling a copy of the *Mercury* that contained the allegedly obscene story "Hatrack." He was now just back from a seven-week tour of the South and the West, during which his pronouncements and activities were chronicled by the press. He had become not merely a leading intellectual figure but something of a celebrity. His opinions and sallies raised hackles in conservative and conventional circles but won him an audience that styled itself as enlightened, sophisticated, disaffected, and up-to-date.

Gretchen Hood was one of this number. She was older than those of the postwar generation who formed the core of Mencken's admirers, but she shared their mood of irreverent liberation. Born on September 15, 1886, she was six years younger than Mencken and had just turned forty. She had seen something of the world and was an independent-minded woman with cosmopolitan tastes. The circumstances of her life were well calculated to engender her enthusiastic response to the freewheeling man of letters.

She grew up in Washington, D.C., where her family had long

resided. Her paternal grandfather, Henry O. Hood, had owned a jewelry store on Pennsylvania Avenue where Abraham Lincoln reportedly used to stop on his walks down the avenue to talk over issues of the day. Her father, Edwin M. Hood, spent almost fifty years in the Washington bureau of the Associated Press and was the first to specialize in covering the State Department and foreign affairs. He was a veteran insider on the Washington scene, respected both by his colleagues of the press and by government and diplomatic officials. He was offered, but refused, an appointment as Assistant Secretary of the Navy in the McKinley administration. He is credited with having suggested to Secretary of State John Hay, as an ultimatum demanding that the Moroccan government secure the release of a kidnapped American citizen, the blunt phrase "Perdicaris alive or Rasuli dead," which became a rallying cry at the 1904 Republican convention renominating Theodore Roosevelt and was popularly believed to have originated with Roosevelt himself. Through Hood, the Wilson administration in early 1917 secretly released the story of the Zimmerman telegram, which helped precipitate America's entry into World War I, and he reported on diplomatic affairs during the whole course of the war and the Versailles peace negotiations. A member of the National Press Club and the Gridiron Club, he was considered the dean of the Washington press corps at the time of his death in 1923.

Edwin Hood's professional life meant that his only child's personal world touched on the public world of journalists, politicians, and diplomats. He was the personal friend of several Secretaries of State from Hay to Charles Evans Hughes, and one, William Jennings Bryan, was a neighbor who dropped in on the Hood family for visits. William Howard Taft and Warren G. Harding were guests at their home. As a newspaperman's daughter, Gretchen Hood had a spectatorial familiarity with the Washington political and social swirl and could look upon it with an amused and detached eye that made her receptive to Mencken's perspective.

Although she lived most of her long life in Washington (she died in 1978), as a young woman she moved well beyond its geographical and social boundaries. Possessed of an excellent soprano voice, she was studying singing and performing as a church soloist when, in 1911, she had a private audition with Madame Ernestine Schumann-Heink. The internationally renowned diva was so impressed that she immediately invited the young singer to come to New York for professional introductions and tryouts. Schumann-Heink's enthusiasm for Hood's vocal gifts was shared by the kappelmeister of the Metropolitan Opera, who urged that she study abroad to prepare herself musically and dramatically for the operatic stage. For the next two years, Hood resided and traveled in Europe, studying in Brussels, Paris, and Nice and gaining exposure to European life and culture in the last years before the war. On occasion, she came in contact with an illustrious society there; she later vividly remembered being embraced on a staircase in Parliament by an "impetuous" Winston Churchill, then First Lord of the Admiralty.

In 1914 she began her professional career in London with the Aborn Opera Company and toured with it in the United States. "By far the most important happening of the Aborn season" in the nation's capital that spring, the *Washington Times* reported, was Hood's operatic debut there. She received an enthusiastic welcome from a standing-room-only audience. Her performance as Marguerite in Gounod's *Faust* drew plaudits from one reviewer for "the wonderful prima donna whom Washington has sheltered all her life." Her claims to "a brilliant future," said another, "lie in the clearness and true musical sweetness of her voice, and in her acting, which bore no trace of the debutante last night, but was charming, full of the grace and ease of an experienced artist, and with a strong individual claim which means personality." [1]

Hood continued to pursue her ambitions on her own, performing with both the San Carlo and the Henry Savage opera companies. She had exchanged a milieu close to public affairs for one dominated by music and the arts. She also tried marriage, but left her husband after little more than a month. Looking back much later on their relationship, she wrote, "If only I had 'tried him out' first I'd never have married him," and she went on to quote Lily Langtry's reply when asked if Edward VII was a romantic lover: "Oh, not at all— just a straight-away pounder." [2]

In 1920 Hood's musical career brought her to New York, where she lived for three years. She gravitated to Greenwich Village, by then well established as a mecca of artistic ferment, intellectual dissent, and bohemian living. While continuing her singing and giving voice lessons, she entered actively into the life that flourished there. She appeared in *A Fantastic Fricasee,* a potpourri of comic songs and

sketches, dance, and puppetry staged at the Greenwich Village Theater in the fall of 1922. She also began writing, first for the short-
lived *Greenwich Villager* and then for the *Quill*. Both magazines were
typical of the little periodicals spawned by the Village, and both were
devoted particularly to celebrating the artistic and intellectual life
that went on there. As editor Bobby Edwards put it, the *Quill*
sought to convince an unbelieving public that the Village was not "a
hoax after all"—that it was "interesting, constructive, inventive, and
to the fugitive from Main Street, nothing short of wonderful."

Hood served as a contributing editor of the *Quill* from September
1922 until October 1924, and for a time she also had charge of advertising. Several items in the magazine casually refer to her as one of
its inner circle, and Edwards did a drawing of her as one of the
"Chickens from the 'Fricasee.'" She reviewed Rafael Sabatini's *Fortune's Fool* and Willa Cather's *A Lost Lady,* and she contributed several poems, the best of which treat the relationship between lovers
from the woman's point of view with a sophistication and ironic
archness in the vein of a lesser Dorothy Parker:

INTERMEZZO

And now that you are gone from me, my dear,
Think not but what I'll faithful be—at least,
"After my fashion" shall we say? Nor East
Nor West shall blow me wind to call a tear;

And whether you come back to me, my dear,
Rests on the knees of all those scheming gods
Who sway your whims, who make of us, the clods
To suffer stupidly—to wait and fear;

And whether you will find, after the year,
(Should you return from fields more fresh, more green)
The same pathetic trust—the slate still clean. . . .
Who knows? . . . . Men come and go, ere then, my dear!

In her poems Hood cultivates an independent sensibility. Working
for the *Greenwich Villager* and the *Quill,* in which art and the artistic
life, psychoanalysis, sexual freedom, and the manners and mores of
Village inhabitants were constant subjects of discussion, she encoun-

tered at firsthand and in ample supply the advocates and doctrines of cultural freedom.[3]

By the time she reached her middle thirties, Hood had worked at making a career for several years, resided by herself in diverse metropolitan settings, tasted marriage briefly, and moved in circles where unconventionality was the order of the day. Then, in 1923, she returned to Washington during her father's final illness and remained there after his death. Why she stayed on is open to conjecture. She surely felt a responsibility to her mother, who was now alone. She probably realized that major success as an opera singer, which had so far eluded her, was not now likely to come about. Possibly she desired a more settled life amid familiar roots. All these things may have played a part in her coming home. Her decision to stay on permanently was not fixed, however, for Mencken's letters show that she wrestled with the idea of leaving again and asked his advice about it.

Whatever her reasons, she chose to live with her mother in the family home at 1226 Fairmont Street N.W., a small row house in a residential neighborhood situated between Howard University to the east and the National Zoological Park to the west and about two miles north of the White House. She began to teach voice with some success; one of her pupils won the 1928 Atwater Kent national radio auditions, and another reached the semifinals the next year. She achieved local celebrity as a concert and radio vocalist, and she sang for Calvin Coolidge and Mrs. Herbert Hoover. She led an active social life, and her circle of friends included a few public figures and others who daily rubbed elbows with them. Yet her interest in the world beyond the nation's capital remained keen, putting the Washington of the Coolidge and Hoover years in perspective. She read not only the *American Mercury* but other journals, as is evident from her calling Mencken's attention to articles she had seen.

She kept in touch, in particular, with the intellectual and cultural scene centered in Manhattan by reading the *New York World*. In the twenties the *World* had a reputation as a national newspaper that appealed to urbane, liberal-minded readers—particularly for its op-ed page, which editor Herbert Bayard Swope originated and filled with a lively mixture of political commentary and cultural reportage. On it, several notable columnists held forth, including Heywood

Broun, Alexander Woollcott, Deems Taylor, and Franklin P. Adams. In a letter to the *World,* dated September 26, 1926, Hood lauded its editorial pages. They had done more than anything else "to open my eyes and direct my thinking. . . . I'd sooner miss my breakfast than miss reading The World. And breakfast to me is the best part of the day. (Perhaps because at that time I read the editorial pages of The World.)" She advocated that they be made compulsory reading in the schools, with the hoped-for effect of transforming "Babbitt-ville."[4] On these pages Hood saw Mencken's *Chicago Tribune* pieces under the title "Hiring a Hall," and through the *World* the lady from Washington first made herself known to the journalist from Baltimore.

Her letter made it clear that her enthusiasm for the *World* was part and parcel of her admiration for Mencken. "It is the naïveté of this country that makes us the laughing-stock of other nations. When the people wake up and realize that such a quality is a menace instead of an asset then and then only will we begin to grow up intellectually. And the way to grow up is to read Mencken and a few others courageous like him." "Too bad," she added, "you can't give him to us every day." On September 27, two days before her letter appeared in the paper, the *World* printed one from Mencken, in which he put forward Senator James A. Reed of Missouri as his choice for the Democratic presidential candidate in 1928. Hood thereupon wrote again to the newspaper with a nomination of her own: "Why not Mencken for President?" She looked to his "uncanny vision," which she implied generated both heat and light, to end the doldrums of "our present system of refrigeration." His "debunking" was the salutary prerequisite to erecting the "magnificent structure" of a genuine civilization in America. The *World* did not print this letter, but forwarded it to Mencken. Upon his return from California two months later, he acknowledged it. He declined to become a candidate, saying he could not take the Constitutional oath so long as the Eighteenth Amendment was law, but Hood dismissed his demurrer. Prohibition would be "automatically annihilated" by his nomination, she wrote him, leaving him no alternative but to run.

Thus began an episode in Mencken's life that has received only passing mention from his biographers. What started as a correspondence between an illustrious personage and an ardent fan developed into a friendship between two individuals with congenial tempera-ments, interests, and tastes. Gretchen Hood's acquaintance with the journalistic life of Washington formed a bond with Mencken, who thought of himself, first and foremost, as an inveterate newspaper-man (they playfully entertained the idea of starting their own Wash-ington newspaper), and she had a ready appreciation for his per-formances as a connoisseur of the Washington political spectacle. Mencken, the amateur musician and music buff, respected her talent and professional background. Even though, as he confessed in *Happy Days,* his love for the art did not extend to opera and he thought of "even the most gifted Wagnerian soprano as no more than a blimp fitted with a calliope," he exempted Hood from his antipathy toward singers.[5] Her mixture of the qualities of a lady at home in Wash-ington society and a free-spirited former habitué of Greenwich Vil-lage undoubtedly added to her attractiveness for Mencken. This combination suited with his own blend of intellectual irreverence and the urbane gentlemanliness he displayed toward the opposite sex. His letters indicate that he found in her an intelligent, witty, and charming respondent to his characteristic traits of personality and style. She both flattered his ego and challenged him to exhibit his celebrated manner at its best. On her part, Hood was not simply awestruck by Mencken's attentions but met them with her indepen-dent verve. "Nothing scared me," she later said of her attitude; "ready to take on all comers." Mencken liked to refer to her as "a licensed outlaw," a designation which captures his impression of her and describes as well the fashionable unconventionality which fueled the Mencken vogue.

Mencken wrote Hood over two hundred letters, and she must have written him about the same number. For much of the time they corresponded, they exchanged several letters every month, some-times as many as four or five a week. As their communications blossomed into a four-year friendship, the flow of letters was soon supplemented by personal meetings. Mencken found occasions to go to Washington to do research at the Library of Congress or to show his niece the sights, and he seized these opportunities to take Hood to the Madrillon, the one restaurant in the city which met his culi-nary standards. She invited him to dine at her home, where they reminisced about the Washington of an earlier time and he drank copious quantities of her home-made beer. He entertained her at

Photograph of Gretchen Hood from the *Washington Times* story in 1927 of her purported romance with Mencken.
(Courtesy of Robert W. Woodruff Library, Emory University)

H. L. Mencken in 1928, working in his "office" at home in Hollins Street. (Courtesy of Enoch Pratt Free Library, Baltimore)

some of his favorite places in Baltimore. When Hood went to New York to visit friends in the summer of 1927, she and Mencken traveled by train together. Several times during her stay, she lunched in his suite at the Algonquin Hotel or dined with him there and afterward went out with him for an evening on the town. On other occasions they planned and staged parties in Washington and Baltimore with great relish.

During the period of their friendship, Mencken shuttled, as he had for many years, between his life in Baltimore and his life in New York. The Baltimore life encompassed three spheres: the red-brick row house at 1524 Hollins Street, where he had grown up and where he now lived with his brother August and his sister, Gertrude; the offices of the *Sunpapers,* where he served as writer, editorial adviser, and resident gadfly; and the haunts where he regularly socialized with Baltimore cronies. His other life revolved around the *American Mercury.* It brought him to Manhattan for a few days every other week or so, where he attended to his editorial chores and stayed at the Algonquin. While he crossed paths occasionally with the literary and journalistic luminaries of the Algonquin Round Table and a variety of other New York celebrities, he usually mingled with his own set of friends, many of whom were contributors to his magazine. When Hood visited the city, he introduced her to Joseph Hergesheimer, Theodore Dreiser, and George Jean Nathan, all longtime literary companions, and to Alexander Woollcott, a fixture at the Round Table.[6] His letters recounted his comings and goings between his two worlds and gave her continual glimpses of the persons who populated them, remarking at one moment on an evening's entertainment in Baltimore and at another on a piece of New York literary gossip. She, in turn, entered into both his worlds with equal zest, whether querying him about writers and articles in the *Mercury* or contributing new stanzas for "I Am a 100% American," the song of his Saturday Night Club in Baltimore.

For the most part, Hood participated vicariously through his letters in Mencken's public combats, but on one occasion she entered the literary lists directly on his behalf. The encounter was sparked by one of Mencken's columns—a caveat against writers' sending endorsements for their work when they submitted it for publication. A bad manuscript, he declared, is invariably accompanied by "a florid letter from the author, detailing his triumphs at high school"; another "from the city editor of the Bingville Bugle certifying that he is the best reporter ever heard of between Cincinnati and Columbus"; and "the inevitable encomiums from the critic of the Jackass (Miss.) Daily News, the Tri-State Confectioner, or the Greenwich Village Libido." Mencken was humorously venting the frustrations of an editor, but his claim that an able writer would find the gates wide open without such aid set off the Greenwich Village author Maxwell Bodenheim. He wrote to the *New York World* that Mencken's assertions about "a vital, often heart-wrenching phase of the literary game" were "so grotesquely inaccurate—to put it mildly—that they require a public contradiction." As proof of what the literary man was up against, Bodenheim singled out his adversary's mock-serious observation that a practical-minded publisher wants for a literary adviser "a Rotarian, and preferably one with experience in the automobile supplies business." Bodenheim contended further that endorsements by certain powerful critics, such as Mencken himself, almost always meant that a book sold well.

Mencken disregarded the assault from one he considered "a poor fish," but Hood answered it in the *World:*

> Maxwell Bodenheim . . . seems to be floundering in a self-inflicted labyrinth, and to have missed the entire purport of Mencken's article. . . .
>
> As I recall it, Mencken dealt with literary attempts before publication, and not after. Therein Mr. Bodenheim fumbles the ball. Mencken's argument was not so much the financial success of a book once it was on sale, bought by a public lured by the recommendations of the mighty literati (which seems to be Mr. Bodenheim's complaint), as the requirements necessary to get the MSS. past the editor's door and into his hands, preferably minus the O.K. of a well-established writer. Briefly, Mencken said all that any MSS. needed was an arresting idea deftly handled, originally wrought, beautifully worded and neatly typed, and it would find its way without trouble to the editor's desk.

In her view, Mencken had "again stated a neglected truth in his ingenious manner, Mr. Bodenheim and other ranking literary opportunists to the contrary." (The adjective she actually used to describe Bodenheim, "rankling," was changed in the published version.) Unmollified, Bodenheim retorted by asking if it was reasonable to assume that those who could assure a book's success *after* publication would not be listened to beforehand; Mencken's defenders, he concluded, were "usually as proficient at sidestepping and evasion as the critic himself." The epistolary duel ended in a standoff, with the two irreconcilable conceptions of the literary situation behind Mencken's witty polemic and Bodenheim's contentious rejoinder largely untouched by the scoring of debater's points that characterized the argument.[7]

Although liberally exposed to Mencken's worlds as a result of their relationship, Hood did not simply gravitate to his orbits. She drew him as well into her life in Washington. In particular, she brought him together with two political figures, each in his own way a colorful counterpart to her literary friend. She first introduced him to the dapper Speaker of the House, Nicholas Longworth. Her hunch that the two men would be congenial proved correct. The scion of a wealthy old Cincinnati family and the husband of Alice Roosevelt Longworth, Theodore Roosevelt's daughter, Longworth had a prominent place in Washington society, yet he held it and his powerful office with amiable aplomb. A profile in the *Mercury* portrayed him as a gentlemanly bon vivant among the bullroarers of the House, with little taste for the public formalities of politics and campaigning but with a zest for life and people. He loved music and played the violin and piano well, was a skilled raconteur, and had an impish sense of humor. These things made him a natural companion for Mencken, as did his fondness for good food and drink, good conversation, and good company.

Mencken found him to be "a thoroughly civilized man," as he wrote after Longworth's death in 1931—"one of the few men of any genuine culture to succeed in politics in our time." And in explaining Longworth's long career in Washington, he came close to describing himself as an observer of the political scene: "To understand him one must always remember that a rogue, to him, was not a sinner to be scorned but a clown to be enjoyed, and that above all other varieties of clowns he loved and cherished the ass political." The Speaker was a staunch Republican regular (only as avowed anti-Prohibitionists were he and Mencken in full accord politically). Yet Mencken exempted him from the derision he heaped on the Harding and Coolidge administrations, primarily because he appreciated the cultivated and lighthearted qualities which made Longworth anything but one of the political stuffed shirts, full of bombast and buncombe, that he delighted in deflating.[8]

Hood also arranged for Mencken to meet Fiorello La Guardia. She had met the then Congressman from East Harlem through Duff Gilfond, the writer who profiled Longworth and also La Guardia for the *Mercury,* and she hatched the idea that he and Mencken would hit it off. She had good reason to think so. Their cocky and ebullient personalities were well matched: the New Yorker wore his Italian-Jewish American background as proudly as the Baltimorean flaunted his German American one; both men savored and excelled at verbal combat and were peerless showmen. Hood probably also saw them as brothers-in-arms, as did Gilfond, whose "La Guardia of Harlem" gave him the look of a Mencken under the Capitol dome.[9] If his stance as a champion of democracy and the little man differed fundamentally from Mencken's outlook, this difference was obscured in the twenties by their common assault against many of the same foes. A liberal and urban maverick in the Republican camp, La Guardia directed his fusillades against the Republican standard-bearers of the day as relentlessly as did Mencken, and he was just as outspoken in his ridicule of the proponents of Prohibition, Anglo-Saxon ascendency, and a business-minded civilization.

Whatever his affinities with La Guardia or Longworth, Mencken's eagerness to socialize with them sprang more from his interest in the woman who put him in their company. As it developed in their letters, of course, their relationship was a private affair, but when they began seeing one another, it caught the attention of the outside world. Very quickly, rumors of romance and impending marriage began to circulate. Mencken's prominence in the public eye, together with his reputation as a confirmed and outspoken bachelor, made him fair game and excellent copy for the press. Interviewers regularly queried him about love and marriage, and he not infrequently expounded his views with characteristic pungency and humor. He was, he told one reporter, "a firm believer in monogamy" who remained single not through any intentional effort on his part but because women knew he would make "an impossible husband." He called falling in love an "intellectual disaster." "A man in full possession of the modest faculties that nature commonly apportions him," he went on, "is at least far enough above idiocy to realize that marriage is a bargain in which he gets the worst of it, even when in some detail or other, he makes a visible gain." In another interview he claimed not to believe that women ever fall in love. "They are far too intelligent to do it." [10] Such utterances provoked curiosity about his relations with the opposite sex, and several stories appeared in the tabloids in these years linking him with one woman or another. His meetings with Hood in New York aroused immediate speculation in the newspapers that he was on the verge of proposing to her. A front-page story in the *Washington Times,* with pictures of both parties, announced—despite Hood's disavowals—that "one of the world's most famous bachelors is said to have fallen at last—and for a Washington girl, too."

The public reports about them had a parallel in their correspondence. Almost from the start, the idea of marriage cropped up in playful form. Having touted Mencken for President, Hood evidently indicated her willingness to campaign as his helpmeet. He, in turn, promised that, provided he could withstand the importunings of a wealthy widow from Hoboken, he would make her his First Lady on the day after his inauguration. From this beginning there grew up between them the fiction of a White House marriage. Embellished by such details as a firstborn son named "Little Otto," a dream about an attempted assassination, and musical evenings at which the President's lady would sing "Die Wacht am Rhine," it runs through the letters as a leitmotif.

Both parties enjoyed indulging in this humorous fantasy. But to what degree did romantic feelings more seriously color their friendship? In Mencken's case, the answer must be inferred from what we know of his relations with other women. Hood, however, later tried to explain her sentiments. "He wasn't a romantic man, in the sense that you'd jump in bed with him. I couldn't imagine him as a lover," she told an interviewer many years later. But she "did want to marry him. We both had a sense of the ridiculous, and I wanted to share that with him." [11] The notes she later attached to Mencken's letters amplify her view. She knew by their second meeting that she wanted to spend the rest of her life with him, she was encouraged in her hopes by things he said, and she believed that the public rumors about them spoiled her chances of winning him. If her attraction to him was not primarily sexual, her emotional attachment and her wish to marry him were nonetheless strong. The depth of her feeling can best be gauged from the hurt and bitterness she confesses to having suffered when she learned he was to marry someone else and from her recurrent references to having lost out to "his protegee" in Baltimore.

Mencken's feelings are another matter. Hood is but one of the women with whom he formed close friendships before and during the twenties. For several years he was deeply interested in Marion Bloom and had thoughts of marriage until, frustrated by his hesitation, she wed another. His acquaintance with film star Aileen Pringle, a frequent companion during his visit to Hollywood in 1926, aroused speculation in the newspapers about a romance and produced an exchange of many letters. Above all, there was Sara Powell Haardt, a young writer and teacher at Goucher College, whom he met in 1923 and eventually married in 1930.

His humorous gibes at love and marriage notwithstanding, Mencken's personal relations with women reflected the high opinion of the opposite sex he voiced in *In Defense of Women* (1918) and other writings. He thoroughly enjoyed their companionship and valued their intelligence and sagacity. Although he dismissed romantic love as simply a matter of hormones getting the better of intelligence, his appreciation of the feminine sensibility was not without its romantic side, expressed in the gallantry, wit, and charm he displayed toward women friends.[12] His letters to Hood provide ample evidence of all these things. But how seriously he entertained the possibility of a deeper attachment is more difficult to ascertain. Whatever his inclinations in this direction, he cloaked them artfully behind the fiction of a presidential marriage to her and behind his epistolary manner.

As with other correspondents, he retained much of his public pose in writing to Hood and seldom expressed his private emotions openly or directly. His way of addressing her, as with most women he liked, is a mixture of outspoken discourse with an intellectual confrère and old-fashioned decorum toward the fair sex. By turns breezy and courtly, this mode defines and delimits the kind of intimacy found in the letters. Any hints of romantic fondness are couched in formal gallantries ("I kiss your hand") or compliments turned with a humorous touch ("Look in the glass! How often do they see such a gal? . . . The Pope himself would begin to wobble"). He obviously found her sexually attractive, and on occasion he indulges in erotic banter through puns and literary allusions. Reading between the lines makes it apparent that Mencken was more than a little taken with Hood, at least for a time, and that he enjoyed immensely the amorous dalliance carried on in their letters and, evidently, when they were together. Yet he stopped short of a forthright commitment. Although he recurrently alluded in his letters to the subject of matrimony and his views on it, often in apparent response to some comment of Hood's, it is unlikely that he seriously contemplated marriage. After some time, as they continued to add to the scenario of their would-be life in the White House, he perhaps suspected that her marital hopes were in earnest and tried indirectly to abate them, all the while maintaining a lighthearted tone: "But would connubial bliss be wise? I have some doubts about it. Wouldn't it be better to go down into history as the only Virgin President ever heard of [?]"

Whatever might have been the case in other circumstances, the fact that Mencken's friendship with Hood did not blossom into a closer union was undoubtedly, as she later surmised, the result of his deepening involvement with Sara Haardt. By the time he began corresponding with Hood, his interest in Haardt, which had begun three years before as that of a fatherly mentor for an aspiring writer and engaging young woman eighteen years his junior, was gradually ripening into love. But the course of their seven-year courtship did not unfold uninterruptedly. Her determination to succeed as a writer, her recurrent bouts with illness, and her strongly independent spirit all held her back from marriage; on his part, Mencken had to dislodge himself from the comfortable grooves in which his bachelor life was firmly set. The obstacles on both sides strained and abridged their growing closeness at various times. They were on "distant terms," according to Sara Mayfield, in the winter of 1926–27, and the following fall Haardt spent three months in Hollywood writing screenplays.

Thus, Mencken's attraction to Hood kindled at a point when his relations with Haardt had temporarily cooled and, subsequently, she was absent from Baltimore for a time. It was during this year that most of his meetings with Hood occurred; thereafter, he saw her only infrequently but kept up the relationship through his letters. His fondness for Hood may well have served to counterbalance his emerging love for Haardt. Hood was not only a comely and intelligent admirer in her own right, but a woman closer to his own age and perhaps, for all her independent demeanor, more willing to move in his reflected light and less insistent on being her own person than was his future wife. For a bachelor approaching fifty, particularly one who prized his single state as Mencken did, cultivating the companionship of both women allowed him to test the waters further without precipitously taking the plunge. When he did, it was with Sara Haardt.

Mencken's letters to Gretchen Hood show his unmistakable epistolary style. They are usually typed but occasionally handwritten, either on his personal half-sheet stationery imprinted with his Hollins Street address or on the aquamarine letterhead of the *American Mercury.* Like most of the many thousands of letters he wrote during his lifetime, they are short and direct, seldom running to more than three or four paragraphs and sometimes no more than a few sentences. They proceed from observation to observation in staccato fashion, often jumping from one subject to another, unrelated one; nothing is lingered over or drawn out in detail. As a body, they constitute a close-up portrait of Mencken at the height of his popular acclaim.

Mencken, the public man, rides several of his favorite hobby horses and delivers a barrage of uninhibited pronouncements on the contemporary scene. He comments candidly on writers and articles in the *Mercury.* He mentions current books as diverse as a French scholar's reflections on modern America and Nan Britton's exposé of her affair with Warren G. Harding. He talks of his own literary endeavors, which are not exempt from his levity; he declares that *Treatise on the Gods,* then in progress, "will be devoted mainly to examining the character and career of God." His discourse reverberates with his impressions of public personalities and his firsthand accounts of important events. Sent to the Pan American Conference early in 1928 as a correspondent for the *Evening Sun,* he finds the diplomatic maneuvers of "the boys in spats" and the bad beer in Havana equally disheartening. Much more to his liking were the quadrennial extravaganzas of electing a President, and his running commentary to Hood on the 1928 campaign from start to finish plays a series of grace notes to his writings about that contest. His unceasing ridicule of Prohibition and tales of his evasions of it enliven the letters, as does the journalist's curiosity about sensational happenings of the moment, such as the Ruth Snyder–Judd Gray murder case. Throughout, we encounter Mencken, the debunker of official American virtues and verities, launching satiric broadsides at his pet targets. Of the antics of certain religious spokesmen, he observes, "the notion that our Heavenly Father has no sense of humor is simply boloney," while he accepts Al Smith's defeat as testimony to "the plain fact . . . that the majority of Americans are Ku Kluxers, and that it is useless to try to beat them by the ballot."

Alongside the image of the public figure, the letters chronicle Mencken's day-to-day life and several personal sides. They capture the texture of his usual round of affairs: his ordinary activities, movements, and concerns; the guests he entertains and the visits he makes to friends; his sitting for a portrait, or building a pergola in his backyard, or entertaining his niece while her mother is in the hospital. We see Mencken as paterfamilias, with his sense of responsibility toward his younger brothers and sister and his attachment to the house in Hollins Street. In his many offhand references, we catch candid looks at a multitude of casual acquaintances and often note, as well, his warm regard and solicitude for close friends. We see, too, his convivial nature and the pleasure he took in congenial company, especially in the eagerness with which he contemplates the parties with Longworth and La Guardia.

Mencken's ingrained habits and tastes are likewise much in evidence. As one music lover to another, he reports to Hood on the performances of the Saturday Night Club and on his annual excursions to the Bach Festival in Bethlehem, Pennsylvania. He speaks often as a self-styled connoisseur of wines and beers. He displays pet crochets, such as his aversion to the automobile. With Hood, as with other correspondents, he shares not only his knowledgeable fascination with medicine and the processes of human physiology, but also his chronic preoccupation with the state of his health. He continually rehearses specific symptoms and describes treatments with a zeal that, in retrospect, led Hood to wonder, "Was ever a man so beset by physical ailments?" Yet his dwelling upon minor ills and waxing lugubrious about his health always have an air of comic exaggeration: "Plainly enough, God is trying to finish both of us. I begin to be afraid to go on the street. Last night an old man hanged himself on a telephone pole behind my house. It is an omen." The same holds true for most of the other poses he strikes—the bon vivant; the philosophical man of the world, proffering advice about life; the aging gentleman, grateful for the attentions of a lovely woman. He immensely enjoys projecting himself as a man of many parts, all of which are enlivened by his irrepressible sense of humor.

We hear in these letters one side of an animated dialogue, filled with clever repartee, fanciful anecdotes and jokes, comic innuendo and wordplay, and Mencken's sheer delight with the American vernacular. He acknowledges praise of his writings with a testimonial: "I ascribe their merit to my life-long use of Father John's Medicine." In Hood's report that she was nearly struck by lightning, he finds a portent: "I begin to suspect that God is engaged in a scheme against us. He let us take comfort in the fact that his aim is commonly very bad." Mencken speaks of indulging himself in "the booze arts," and refers to the aftereffects of his annual bout with hay fever as the "sequelae of catarrhus aestivus." A newspaper item about their supposed romance provokes the remark, "The Washington Times certainly done us noble." Even small touches communicate the fascination he finds in words themselves. He obviously enjoys using idiosyncratic variations, like "kaif" and "kaffy" for a cafe or restaurant, or employing the lengthy chemical names for drugs. Postcards from his travels parody the tourist's clichés with their ubiquitous "swell": "Every town is more swell than either other. Everybody is doing their best to show me a swell time."

Mencken's joking with his correspondents extended to his habit of enclosing various items in his letters. Among the things he sent Hood were a Bible tract on modern women's dress, headed "As It Was in the Days of Sodom"; a postal telegram brochure offering sixteen ready-made Christmas greetings; and a form to express regrets for "Breaches of Etiquette," with a checklist of offenses. He also sent printed hoaxes of his own devising: a flyer for the Tobacco-Chewer's Protective and Educational League of America, and cards advertising Ming Aaron's Kosher Chinese restaurant or the services of the Reverend I. Mandolowitz for everything from weddings, funerals, and Hebrew lessons to collecting rents and repairing sewing machines. On one occasion, Mencken passed on to Hood a letter sent to him by a man from Tompkins Corners, New York, facetiously protesting "the growing aggressiveness of the 'gentler sex.'" Describing himself as past fifty, a widower, and not overly prudish, the writer professed to having been nevertheless discomfited when, on a recent train trip, a young woman of eighteen or nineteen suddenly intruded into his Pullman berth with the admonition, "If you do not give me what I want, I'll scream." Mencken solicited Hood's advice on the matter with mock solemnity: "Can't something be done to help the author of the enclosed letter? I should think Congress would move in the matter."

At times, however, when Mencken counsels Hood on personal matters, he strikes a more serious note of consideration and concern. He is especially regardful of her mother, who from their first meeting, according to her daughter, became his "subject for life." His inquiries and well-wishes concerning Mrs. Hood can likely be ascribed to what William Manchester has characterized as Mencken's extravagant gallantry with elderly women. His apologies for the distress the gossip in the press about her daughter may have caused her evince his strong sense of propriety where private affairs and personal sensibilities were concerned. His deference toward her recalls his devotion to his own mother and his painful sense of loss upon her recent death in December 1925. Having lived with Anna Mencken for all of his adult life until she died, Mencken felt an affinity with Hood's situation. When she considered leaving Washington, he understood that she was torn between her duty to her mother and her sense of missed opportunities for herself. Offering his own example as a parallel, he made himself a sounding board for her divided feelings, alternately acknowledging her desire for an independent life and admonishing her that she would be unhappy apart from her mother. One may wonder whether, as a man, Mencken was able to empathize wholly with Hood's dilemma, for his own case, of course, was different. Having at an early age assumed the responsibilities of the head of the family at the death of his father in 1898, he had succeeded in fashioning an extraordinary career of national dimensions without disturbing his domestic life in Baltimore. Given the prevailing expectations and presuppositions about men and women in American society, Hood undoubtedly found it much more difficult to resolve the conflicting claims of filial loyalty and professional independence and success. Yet if Mencken was unable to put himself completely in her place, his sympathetic efforts to commiserate with her and advise her were nonetheless genuine.

A less engaging and more problematic side of Mencken surfaces as well in these letters, one that raises questions about his attitudes toward certain groups and that has laid him open to charges of racial prejudice. Here as elsewhere he sprinkles his correspondence with such terms as "coon," "kike," or "wop" that grate uncomfortably on even admiring present-day readers, and his offhand gibes at different peoples sometimes cross the line between humorous raillery and offensive slurs. Such utterances give some substance to the view that he was, at the very least, crassly insensitive and, at most, a bigot. Accusations of this sort, especially that he was anti-Semitic, have more than once been leveled against him, particularly after his persistent failure in the 1930s to fathom the malignity of Hitler's Germany. Most of the people who knew him best, however, have defended him, affirming that his personal dealings with others were altogether unmarred by such prejudices and pointing to instances in the public record where he denounced or derided discriminatory practices and inhumane acts against blacks or Jews.[13]

The fact is that the whole gamut of Mencken's diverse responses to minority groups and their situation in American society reveals a complicated sensibility that resists categorical judgments. One cannot candidly gainsay that many of Mencken's remarks about Jews or Italians or black Americans are demeaning—as are, for example, the "Polish jokes" of our own day. On the other hand, such evidence does not mean that he disliked the members of this or that group—any more than anyone who has ever told or laughed at a "Polish joke" can therefore be said to dislike Poles or Polish Americans. Part of the explanation for Mencken's habit of expressing himself as he did is that he lived and wrote in a time when hierarchical notions of racial differences still had wide intellectual (as well as popular) currency and when racial and ethnic badinage, stereotypes, and labels were an accepted commonplace of American life and humor. Undeniably, this cultural climate colored his outlook. In this context, Mencken's comments were less glaring than they now appear.

But there is more to it than his being simply a creature of his time. For one thing, the vernacular terms he applied to all sorts of groups reflect the pleasure he took in the American language. He clearly enjoyed such words of and for themselves, quite apart from their pejorative connotations. For another thing, his use of them was intended to be funny and needs to be seen as part of his proclivities as a writer toward humor and satire. What derogatory intent he had was almost certainly tied to his general outlook on his fellow humans: for him, the human species, aside from a few individuals of superior mind and talent, consisted of the vast, unthinking "booboisie" which he made the chief butt of his humor. From this perspective, disparaging racial or national designations did not have their more usual import of singling out a particular stock as outside or inferior to the human norm. Rather, in common with other designations that lumped people together, they more nearly accorded with Mencken's conception of that norm. His criticism scorched almost every conceivable group; he found none more opprobrious than the "Anglo-Saxons," in both their English and American branches, and even his strong Germanophilia did not entirely exempt the Germans as targets. In this light, his use of derisive racial epithets was of a piece with his use of "wowser," "pedagogues," "Bible Belt," "sub-Potomac yokels," and the like as but another reflection of his low opinion of the general run of humankind. One comes close to the heart of Mencken's way of seeing human groups and group behavior in a brief observation he made to Hood: "The coons may be bad, but they are better than whites."

One letter, in particular, sheds fuller light on Mencken's personal attitudes toward the struggle of black Americans. Hood evidently wrote him that black families were moving, or trying to move, into her neighborhood. He responded that he faced the same situation on Hollins Street. For himself, he said it made no difference. Yet because he knew it upset his mother, he had hired a lawyer to draw up a restrictive agreement which most of his fellow homeowners signed. He advised Hood that her neighbors might follow the same course. This story reveals how split Mencken's feelings were about the matter. It highlights the similar ambivalence that marks his Monday articles around this time on a changing Baltimore.

When he looked at the transformation of once white neighborhoods into black ones, he sympathized with the understandable desire of black Baltimoreans who sought to escape the alleys and enjoy better circumstances "they have well earned." But this sympathy balanced uneasily against his sensitivity to the plight of white homeowners who had sunk their life's savings into their houses, "only to find their property ruined and their contentment destroyed by the Negro invasion." His fundamental belief in individual liberty and his predilections as a cosmopolitan man of letters made Mencken sympathetic to the efforts of black Americans to achieve their rightful dignity and place in this society. Yet he nonetheless remained, as Gwin Owens has observed, a son of late nineteenth-century middle-class Baltimore with its "acquired prejudices." These prejudices are plainly evident in his unguarded remarks to Hood. Black families had long lived in the alley behind Hollins Street, and their children were among his boyhood playmates. But black property owners on the street were another matter. His strong attachment to the style of life in which he had grown up, his emotional aversion to almost any changes in the familiar environs of his beloved Baltimore, and, above all, his deep loyalty to his mother obviously in this case outweighed all other sentiments.[14]

His correspondence with Gretchen Hood, then, shows both the public figure and the individual man from several angles. He writes as the famous editor from New York, but as much or more as the affable gentleman from nearby Baltimore. Each in its own way is a persona that bespeaks him yet, at the same time, allows him to maintain a certain personal reticence beneath his cordial frankness. The perspective resulting from his writing extensively to a single correspondent over a short span of time brings the Mencken of the late twenties into sharp focus, revealing with particular immediacy the man the *New York Times* in 1927 called "the most powerful private citizen in America."

The end came suddenly. On August 7, 1930, five days after the announcement had appeared in the *Baltimore Sun*, Mencken wrote Hood, "I suppose you have heard of my approaching marriage." Although the number of letters had dropped off during the past year, there had been no change in their matter or manner that indicated the step he was contemplating. Only once in his letters had he ever spoken of Sara Haardt—a passing mention of her having to undergo surgery, which must have seemed to Hood no more than another of his many references to his acquaintances' ailments. By her own account, she was unprepared for "the worst shock I ever had." Mencken's casual disclosure kept up the facetious note of all his earlier allusions to marriage, harking back to his initial profession that a rich widow was out to catch him. Perhaps he was attempting to let Hood down easily. Perhaps, and this is more likely, he never properly gauged the nature of her feelings and failed to realize how much his news might hurt her.

In any case, her hopes were dashed, and his way of informing her left her bitter. This bitterness still lingered when, over thirty years later, she appended her notes to his letters. Yet, at the time, she hid her true feelings behind a banter that matched his own. As she remembered it, she replied simply that she wished him to be "the most militantly happy husband in captivity." She requested, with tongue in cheek, to sing "You Promised Me" at the wedding (perhaps, too, there was veiled sarcasm, if she intentionally mistitled the familiar wedding song). When Mencken responded by asking her to sing their song, "Die Wacht am Rhein," it must have been the final blow.

Their correspondence had a brief coda five years later, after Sara Haardt Mencken's death. Hood sent Mencken her condolences, and his reply was the first of four more letters. In each, he spoke of getting together again soon, but he does not appear to have pushed it. On her part, though this did not at first stop her from writing, Hood insisted that she was "too completely 'done in' even after 5 years" to see him again. Mencken's active literary and journalistic life, and his prolific correspondence with friends, continued until November 1948, when he suffered a stroke which left him unable to read or write. He died in his Hollins Street home in 1956. Hood lived on in Washington until 1978, when she died at the age of ninety-one. Their relationship, however, was never rekindled. Mencken's last letter, early in 1937, recaptured something of the spirit of those written before he married, but Hood never answered it. "The end," she penciled on the envelope.

Notes to Introduction

Various sources besides her notes with Mencken's letters have yielded information about Gretchen Hood's family and life. See especially Donald P. Baker, "Oh So Sincerely, H. L. Mencken," *Washington Post,* 24 June 1973, "Potomac" sec., pp. 18–19, 32, 35, and obituaries in *Washington Post,* 3 May 1978, pp. A1, A17, and *New York Times,* 3 May 1978, p. B2. On Edwin Hood, see obituaries in *Washington Evening Star,* 9 Aug. 1923, p. 7, and *New York Times,* 10 Aug. 1923, p. 11; *Goldfish Bowl* [newsletter of the National Press Club], 4, nos. 31–33, March, May, July 1937; Oliver Gramling, *AP: The Story of News* (New York: Farrar and Rinehart, 1940), pp. 188–89, 256–61. On Gretchen Hood's operatic career, see clippings from *Musical American,* 25 Nov. 1911; *New York Telegraph,* 11 July 1914; *Washington Evening Star,* 31 May 1914, 7 June 1914, 9 June 1914, 11 March 1915, 14 March 1915, in Gretchen Hood File, Library of the Performing Arts, Lincoln Center, New York.

1. *Washington Times* (Gardner Mack), 9 June 1914, p. 7; *Washington Post* (unsigned), 9 June 1914, p. 5.

2. Hood's note with Mencken's letter of 8 July 1927.

3. Edwards's editorial appeared in June 1922 (p. 7), Hood's poem in Sept. 1922 (p. 22).

4. Clipping of published letter in Mencken/Hood Collection.

5. (New York: Alfred A. Knopf, 1940), p. 195.

6. Hood's note with Mencken's letter of 20 April 1927.

7. Mencken's column appeared in the *World* on June 12, 1927. Bodenheim's letter attacking it appeared on June 19; Hood's answer on June 27; and Bodenheim's rejoinder to her on July 5.

8. Duff Gilfond, "Mr. Speaker," *American Mercury* (Aug. 1927), pp. 451–58; Mencken, "One Who Will Be Missed," *American Mercury* (Sept. 1931), pp. 35–36.

9. *American Mercury* (June 1927), pp. 152–58. La Guardia's biographer, Arthur Mann, finds the resemblance apt in several respects, in *La Guard-*

ia: A Fighter against His Times, 1882–1933 (Philadelphia: Lippincott, 1959), pp. 183–86.

10. Interview with Hannah Stein, [Philadelphia] *Public Ledger,* 18 Dec. 1927, magazine sec., p. 5; "Mencken: Romantic Love Is the Bunk," *Washington Daily News,* 13 March 1928, p. 16.

11. Baker, "Oh So Sincerely," p. 32.

12. Carl Bode tells the story of Mencken's attachment to Marion Bloom in *Mencken,* and prints several of Mencken's letters to her in the *New Mencken Letters.* Bode's *Mencken* also gives the fullest account of Mencken's association with Aileen Pringle, and recounts episodes with Beatrice Wilson and Anita Loos. All of Mencken's biographers treat his romance with Sara Haardt, but none chronicles it with more detailed and personal insight than Sara Mayfield in *The Constant Circle;* a good friend to the other Sara, Mayfield was close to both her and Mencken during much of the period of their courtship. The best discussion of Mencken's views on women, sex, and marriage is in Charles Fecher's *Mencken: A Study of His Thought.* Mencken's biographers have paid almost no attention to Gretchen Hood; Bode mentions her briefly, while in *Disturber of the Peace* William Manchester refers to her simply as an unnamed "Washington opera singer."

13. For recent discussions of this thorny matter, see Fecher, pp. 99n, 181n, 214–17; Alistair Cooke, *Six Men* (New York: Alfred A. Knopf, 1977), pp. 109–10; Joseph Epstein, "Rediscovering Mencken," *Commentary,* 63 (April 1977), 47–52; Robert Kanigel, "Did H. L. Mencken Hate the Jews?" *Menckeniana,* #73 (Spring 1980), 1–7; Gwin Owens, "Mencken and the Jews, Revisited," *Menckeniana,* #74 (Summer 1980), 6–10.

14. I have not found any evidence outside this letter that Mencken initiated the agreement he mentions. However, particularly in view of the reference to his mother, it is unlikely that he fabricated the story for Hood's benefit. He publicly spoke to the Baltimore situation in "Smoke" and "Changing Baltimore" (*Baltimore Evening Sun,* 7 May and 17 Dec. 1928). On several occasions throughout his career, Mencken attacked the unjust and inhuman treatment of black persons, whether it took the form of raw brutality or polite discrimination. A lynching on Maryland's Eastern Shore in 1931 moved him to excoriate the community sentiment that condoned it, just as a few years earlier the refusal of a Baltimore hotel to permit Countee Cullen to address a luncheon there aroused his scorn. As editor of the *Mercury,* he published and expressed admiration for such

black writers as James Weldon Johnson, Kelly Miller, and Walter White, and he made something of a protégé of the black journalist George Schuyler. As a critic, his judgments of black Americans' achievements in the arts, as Heywood Broun remarked even while challenging some of them, stemmed from his consideration of the work of black artists on an equal footing with all other artists, not as a special case ("It Seems to Heywood Broun," *Nation,* 19 Oct. 1927, pp. 416–17). The importance of Mencken in relation to the Harlem Renaissance has recently been explored in Charles Scruggs, *The Sage in Harlem: H. L. Mencken and the Black Writers of the 1920's* (Baltimore and London: Johns Hopkins University Press, 1984).

Editorial Note

The present selection includes, in chronological order, the complete texts of 136 letters and two postcards from the 248 communications which Mencken sent Hood. In addition, two telegrams and passages from other letters are quoted in the notes. I have not included those letters which largely recapitulate others that appear herein, simply confirm engagements mentioned elsewhere, or are otherwise incidental. I have also left out some postcards, telegrams, and greeting cards, as well as items Mencken sent Hood without an accompanying letter—a newspaper clipping, some of Upton Sinclair's blurbs for his publications, and an invitation to Mencken to inspect a new steamship of the North German Lloyd line. In my judgment, the omitted items add little to the record presented here of this episode in Mencken's life.

I have not tried to reproduce the originals exactly as each appears, but have used a consistent format that corresponds closely to the look of Mencken's letters. The type of communication is indicated in brackets at the upper left of each letter:

[TLS]   typed letter, signed by hand
[ALS]   autograph letter, signed by hand
[APS]   autograph postcard, signed by hand

The place of origin is shown on the letterhead, where there is one; otherwise, the place of postmark is given in brackets. When the letterhead and the postmark are not the same, both places are given, with the latter in brackets. The two letterheads which appear on the bulk of the letters are not reproduced in full. The letterhead of Mencken's personal stationery—"H. L. Mencken 1524 Hollins St. Baltimore."—is designated simply as "Baltimore." Likewise, that of the *American Mercury* is designated simply as "New York." (The complete letterhead reads: "*The American Mercury* 730 Fifth Avenue New York" beneath the magazine's logotype, and shows the names of

Mencken as editor, Alfred A. Knopf as publisher, and Samuel Knopf as business manager, as well as the cable address and telephone number of the magazine.) In other cases, the letterhead is given with the individual letter.

The date appears as it does on the original letter. When this date is partial, the omissions are added in brackets. When a letter has no date or when the date is questionable in light of the postmark date, the latter is also given in brackets or a note.

The texts retain the wording, spelling, and punctuation of the originals, except where emendations seem called for to make clear the sense. In such instances, corrections are made in brackets. Uncertain words in holograph letters are followed by a question mark in brackets. I have silently corrected obvious typographical errors, such as misspacings, run-together words, and superimposed characters. Placement of the closing and the signature has been regularized, and Mencken's handwritten closings, which do not render clearly all the letters of "Sincerely yours" or "Yours," are written out in full to correspond to his typed closings. All postscripts and marginalia appear below the signature, regardless of where they are located in the original.

A long while after their correspondence ended, Hood wrote quite a few notes to Mencken's letters. Her comments and observations give a sense of her personality, her reactions to Mencken, and her view of her relationship with him. Most of her notes are in pencil on 3-by-5-inch sheets and are attached to individual letters. Almost all are undated, but two of the last notes show "June 22—1964" and an earlier one refers to Jacqueline Kennedy as the First Lady, suggesting that all of these notes were probably written in the early sixties. Hood added a few more notations, in pencil or in ink, to Xerox copies which were later made of the letters and her 3-by-5 notes.

No attempt has been made to reproduce Hood's notes in their entirety, for they are often repetitious. I have drawn on them in the introductory essay and have cited the more significant ones, in full or in part, with the letters. Those notes which pertain to a letter as a whole or provide a context for it follow immediately after the letter in question and are designated by the initials *G.H.* Occasionally, a note is not placed with the letter to which Hood attached it, either because that letter has been omitted from this collection or because the note refers more directly to the letter to which it is appended here. Those notes which simply identify persons or things are quoted or paraphrased in the footnotes. I have retained the abbreviations, spelling, and punctuation (or omissions of punctuation) in Hood's notes, unless corrections were necessary for clarity. Such corrections appear in brackets.

My annotation of the letters has been carried out with two purposes in mind: first, to identify persons, places, things, or events that may not be readily known to readers who are not thoroughly acquainted with Mencken; second, to clarify and amplify the purport of significant items within the letters themselves or related to their immediate context. Certain of Mencken's oblique or elliptical remarks to Hood can be better understood when the background for them is made evident. In explaining or enlarging upon matters he brings up with Hood, I have used Mencken's own words as much as possible, quoted from published pieces written at or close to the same time as the letters and sharing the same ambiance. When my explanation of something is conjectural, I have based it on as much concrete evidence as I could uncover, and in such cases I have acknowledged the element of uncertainty in my interpretation. Inevitably, those who know Mencken's life and writings may find some of the notes unnecessary; but I trust that, in the main, these commentaries will enhance the reader's enjoyment of the letters by making references more meaningful and by enriching the import of the correspondence as it illuminates both the friendship between Mencken and Hood and Mencken's career during these years.

Numerous and varied sources yielded information for the annotations and the introduction, but certain ones deserve special mention: two biographies of Mencken, William Manchester's *Disturber of the Peace: The Life of H. L. Mencken* (New York: Harper [1950]) and Carl Bode's *Mencken* (Carbondale: Southern Illinois University Press, 1969); the two general collections of Mencken's letters, *Letters of H. L. Mencken,* ed. Guy J. Forgue (New York: Alfred A. Knopf, 1961) and *The New Mencken Letters,* ed. Carl Bode (New York: Dial Press, 1977); Charles Fecher, *Mencken: A Study of His Thought* (New York: Alfred A. Knopf, 1978); Sara Mayfield, *The Constant Circle: H. L. Mencken and His Friends* (New York: Delacorte Press, 1968); and Betty Adler's splendid *H. L. M.: The Mencken Bibliography* (Baltimore: Johns Hopkins University Press, 1961).

The Letters

[TLS] New York [Baltimore]
December 6, 1926

Dear Miss Hood:
  The editor of the *World* sends me your letter of October 4.
Unluckily I find it impossible to accept the nomination. How could
I make oath to support the Eighteenth Amendment?

Sincerely,

H. L. MENCKEN

Gretchen Hood had written the *New York World:*

> Why not Mencken for President? The idea has been gather-
> ing momentum in my head for several months. Think of erudi-
> tion in the White House coupled with fearless ability! At least
> the experiment promises excitement —anything but our pres-
> ent system of refrigeration. Here is a man with uncanny vision
> in all directions, who can anticipate the needs of our country
> ten—twenty—fifty years hence. He sees further than right un-
> der his nose. What to discard and what to use; what is impor-
> tant and what is drivel: is not so keen a sense of values the first
> implement with which to begin to debunk America?
>   As for those loyal citizens, Mr. Mencken, who are indulging
> in the grandiose gesture of protecting the poor country from
> your enlightening onslaughts, all I can say is: go on, Mr. Menc-
> ken, and let 'em be noble if they want! Just you be yourself!
>   After the debunking there must arise a magnificent struc-
> ture, but first do the debunking. You've started. Don't quit!

On December 8, 1926, Miss Hood replied to Mencken's letter:

Dear Mr. Mencken:

Regarding my letter to the World of Oct 4, and yours to me of Dec 6: Can you not see that if you are nominated there will be no 18th Amendment? It will be automatically annihilated. The gray matter in the heads of the people who will nominate you will attend to the killing of so dangerous and jackass a law.

So there's nothing for you to do but accept the nomination—

Sincerely—no, stronger than that—

Enthusiastically yours
GRETCHEN HOOD

(Handwritten copies of both letters, on Hood's personal stationery, are in the Mencken/Hood Collection.)

[TLS]

New York [Baltimore]
December 29, 1926.

Dear Miss Hood:

You put me in a very unfavorable position. I have already promised faithfully to support two different candidates, Senator Reed, and Governor Ritchie, and now you tempt me to turn traitor to both of them.[1] I shall go into prayer upon the subject.

Sincerely yours,

H. L. MENCKEN

1. In a letter to the *New York World,* which probably called forth Hood's letter nominating him, Mencken declared that, unlike either of the presumed front-runners, Al Smith or William Gibbs McAdoo, Reed could unite the Democratic Party in 1928. "What a campaign he would make. And what a charming novelty it would be to see in the White House a man who was at once competent, courageous, honest, plain-spoken—and a gentleman!" ("A Nomination by Mr. Mencken," 27 Sept. 1926, editorial page). Mencken was also promoting the candidacy of another friend, Governor Albert C. Ritchie of Maryland.

[ALS]   New York
                                     [January 5, 1927]

Dear Miss Hood:
   It would be very charming, but I fear that you'd starve to death
before 1932. But if luck were with us maybe I'd be able to make
enough money in the stock market! Meanwhile, I am consulting
my pastor!

                                     Sincerely yours

                                     H. L. MENCKEN

[TLS]   New York [Baltimore]
                                     January 14, 1927

Dear Miss Hood:
   Very well. Put your magicians to work. If I go into the White
House on March 4, 1932—I hereby promise and negotiate to marry
you with bell and book on March 5.[1] That is, provided I am not
already married to a rich widow in Hoboken who now has at me.[2]

                                     Yours,

                                     H. L. MENCKEN

1. He means 1933.
2. Mencken responded characteristically to the rumors that circulated about
   him and various women by inventing the story of his engagement to
   Bertha Kupfernagel, a widow from Hoboken well endowed financially
   and otherwise.

[T L S]   New York [Baltimore]
                                            January 17th [1927]

Dear Miss Hood:—

I wish I could get to the ball, but it will be impossible. But there
will be a stupendous Inaugural Ball on March 4, 1933, and I
promise to dance until I am winded.

                              Sincerely yours,

                              H. L. MENCKEN

[T L S]   Baltimore
                                            February 23rd [1927]

Dear Miss Hood:—

You touch me on a tender spot when you speak of that scene in
"Heliogabalus".[1] I wrote it almost in sobs. It is astounding how
sentimental a decaying man can be. But let us not compromise. To
hell with the Presidency! I am a candidate for Emperor.

I am amazed that you should raise any doubts about my chastity.
It is one of the marvels of the modern world. If I had sacrificed it I
might have been a star in the movies by now.

Do you ever come to Baltimore to shop? If so, why not have
lunch with me? The victualry here is pretty good, and the Volstead
Act is unheard of.

I am trying to start a new book, and making very heavy weather
of it.[2] The labor pains in such cases are always severe.

                              Sincerely yours,

                              H. L. MENCKEN

G.H.: *"He was beginning to grow curious. I had never told him anything about myself—whether I took in dish washing & scrubbing—that I
was an opera singer, . . . nothing. Later, when I reminded him that he'd
written unkind things about singers & he had actually heard me sing, he
soothed me by saying: 'Oh, but you are a licensed outlaw—you can get
away with anything!'"*

1. A risqué farce set in imperial Rome, coauthored by Mencken and George Jean Nathan in 1919 and published in 1920. Gretchen Hood does not identify "that scene," but the banter about marriage in previous letters suggests it may well have been the climax of Act I, in which the reprobate emperor forswears his eleven wives to wed a demure and fetching Christian maiden.

2. At this time, Mencken was beginning a study of religion that eventually became *Treatise on the Gods* (1930), and he was also pursuing a project called "Homo Sapiens," which he never completed.

[TLS]   Baltimore
                                                March 2nd [1927]

Dear Miss Hood:—

Hell, no! The new book will certainly *not* defend democracy! It will be a general slaughter of the human race. I hope to start it week after next. I'll have to come to your great city now and then to hunt material in the Library of Congress. I pray to God that you will be kind, and have lunch with me then. And that you will be in Baltimore some time before. Give me a day's notice if you can. I'll be here all of this week, and next week after Thursday; then for two weeks running.

I lament the necessity of warning you that stroking their skulls does authors no good when they are at work. What they really need is regular meal service, with now and then a drink and a kind word. I speak of the males. What the ladies use to keep up their courage I don't know, but have often wondered. Maybe they secretly smoke cigars.

                                        Sincerely yours,

                                        H. L. MENCKEN

G.H.: "*I made up my mind not to go to Balt. first. Rather nervy, and lacking in awe of America's greatest—the most!—but I was ever thus. Nothing scared me—ready to take on all comers.*"

[ALS]

Hotel Algonquin
New York
[March 6, 1927]

Dear Miss Hood:

I'll be in Washington next Sunday afternoon, for a couple of hours' work in the Library of Congress. Will you have dinner with me? I'll escape from the Library at about 6 p.m. Will you let me know at Baltimore? I'll be back there by Thursday.

That 7% beer arouses all my worst instincts. I bespeak a two-gallon carboy of it.[1]

Some copies of the Woollcott song are on their way to you.[2] You may have as many more as you want. I have had an electrotype made

Sincerely yours

H. L. MENCKEN

1. Gretchen Hood's home brew. *G.H.:* "The first time he came to dinner here he drank *15* bottles & *never had to go upstairs once.* What a man! But he sure loved my beer—came back often. Later, when Ed Kemler phoned me (this was after HLM married) & asked for an interview to get a few anecdotes etc for the biography he was writing about HLM, I replied: 'You may say that he was not interested in *me*—only in the superb beer I brewed.' This was soon after the marriage: I was very bitter then—more bitter than the beer I'd brewed. Never shook it off." (Edgar Kemler began to write his book in 1946, sixteen years after Mencken's marriage and eleven years after Sara Mencken's death. *The Irreverent Mr. Mencken* [1950] does not mention Hood.)

2. William W. (Willie) Woollcott, a Baltimore manufacturer and brother of author and critic Alexander Woollcott, was a nonperforming member of Mencken's musical circle, the Saturday Night Club. His song, "I Am a One Hundred Percent American," is a rollicking lampoon in a thoroughly Menckenesque vein:

> I am a one, I am a one,
> I am a one hundred percent American;
> I am a supe, I am a supe,
> I am a super patriot;
> A red, red, red, red, red I am,
> A red blooded American;
> I am a one hundred percent American, I am, God damn, I am!

The piece was a club standby, to which new stanzas, by various hands, were continually added. (Copy of sheet music with handwritten notation, "Did I send you this? HLM," in Mencken/Hood Collection.)

[T L S]   Baltimore
                                           Thursday [March 10, 1927]

Dear Miss Hood:—

I have just got in from New York, and find your letter. I'll finish
at the library about 5.30 on Sunday. Wouldn't it be safest for me to
call for you at your house? If we planned to meet somewhere else
we might miss each other. But if you prefer to meet downtown I
suggest the Madril[l]on restaurant. I don't know the address, but it
is near the Treasury, and you can find it. I suggest 6 P.M. Will you
let me know as above? I'll introduce myself to the proprietor, and if
you ask for me he will find me.

Are you still looking for coherance in sermons?[1] For shame! It is
the privilege of the rev. clergy to talk like damned fools.

Yours,

H. L. MENCKEN

---

1. Probably alludes to a sermon preached by the Reverend John Haynes
Holmes at the Community Church in New York City on Sunday, February 27, 1927. Viewing Mencken as the "contemporary prophet" of the
disillusioned young, Holmes applauded his courageous spirit of revolt,
but rejected his philosophy as cynical, defeatist, and anarchistic: "If Mr.
Mencken himself should change, if he should inform himself with respect
to the things he has neglected and misunderstood, if he should find it in
his heart to pity man in his struggle, if he should employ his great gifts in
the service of humankind, he would take his place among the great proph-
ets of all time. He must change." ("Mencken Held Up as Seer of Revolt,"
New York World, 28 Feb. 1927, p. 5. Clipping in Mencken/Hood
Collection.)

On March 11, 1927, Gretchen Hood wrote Mencken:

Dear Mr. Mencken:

Yes, come to my house for me, when you finish at the
Library. We must make it respectable, by all means. You're
right, it will be safest & avoid possible confusion.

I had a hunch you'd select the Madril[l]on—saw the letter
you wrote to Peter Borras.

Of course you expect me to have a gang here at my house to meet you when you call for me? Sorry, but I can't grant you that, much as you crave it. I refuse to share you with anybody.

Yours selfishly,
GRETCHEN HOOD

In response to a diatribe by Mencken against the restaurants in the nation's capital, Peter Borras, the proprietor of the Madrillon, invited him to dine there. After sampling the cuisine, Mencken wrote Borras: "I congratulate you on your solitary eminence in a city of bad victuals." (Newspaper clipping, untitled and undated, in Mencken/Hood Collection.)

[ALS]   Baltimore
                                         [March 14, 1927]

God will reward you for being so charming to an aged man. I only hope you let me come back very soon. I was in a low state yesterday, but you bucked me up. Don't forget to send that new stanza for the Woollcott song![1] I'll add it to the next edition.

Yours,

HLM

G.H.: "*The spread at the Madril[l]on was fit for Lucullus! HLM bounced in here, handed over 2 bottles of rare wines to mother which floored her & made her a subject for life. I recall, I wore a delft blue velvet dress (incidentally, my* wedding *dress 1914, made over) which caught his eye at once. What a talker he was—I never got in a word edgewise, just sat, engrossed & enthralled & heard his life story. Later, I took him to the home of the Leon Ulmans (she was pal from girlhood) played & sang for him some German & French songs he enjoyed—then drove down in taxi & put him on train for Balt. He kissed me fervently many times & promised to see me soon.*"

1. Hood sent Mencken three stanzas she wrote for "I Am a One Hundred Percent American" (copies in Mencken/Hood Collection):

> I am a cur, I am a cur,
> I am a curfew-ringing Holier-than-thou;
> I'll not demur, I'll not demur
> If all our pleasures die right now;
> For folks who work hard thro' the day
> Shall never have the night to play,
> I am a 100% etc.
>
> I am a stick, I am a stick,
> I am a stickler for the proper and the smug;
> I get a kick—I get a kick
> When I suppress a kiss or hug;
> For virtue driven to excess
> Brings sexy dreams of righteousness
> I am a 100% etc.
>
> I am a bum—I am a bum
> I am a bumptious, talky, Europe-going pest;
> I strike 'em dumb—I strike 'em dumb
> When I perform at their request;
> Of our pre-eminence I bray—
> I dare 'em to love the U. S. A.
> I am a 100% etc.

[TLS]   Baltimore
                                         March 26th [1927]

Dear Miss Hood:—

Today is the 100th anniversary of old Ludwig's death. I pause in my accustomed round of duties, repair to my respective house of worship, and give him three bawdy cheers. What a man!

Tonight the club will sing the following in his honor:

> I am a beat,
> I am a beat,
> I am a beat-o-venish fan and connysoor,
> And I can eat,
> And I can eat,

And I can eat his music up.
Three cheers for Ludwig; he's a match
For Wagner, Sousa, Brahms and Bach.
    I am a one, etc.

Yours,

H. L. Mencken

I leave the redecoration of the White House, in 1932, to you. But put in a good bar!

[TLS]   Baltimore
March 28th [1927]

Dear Miss Hood:—
    The dinner sounds perfect. Next Sunday, unfortunately, I'll have to be in New York, and maybe God will be kind and polite enough to let me come Sunday a week. Will that be convenient? I'll come over early in the afternoon, and slave in the Library a few hours. This book-writing is no easy job. I sometimes wish I had gone in for statecraft instead.
    You are a superb guesser. I was born on September 12th, far back in the last century. General Grant was still alive, and women still wore bustles. I knew Washington very well as a boy, but chiefly the saloons. My father had a wide acquaintance with them. His talents I inherit.
    Clarence Darrow was here all day yesterday.[1] He'll be 70 in two weeks, but he seem younger than I am.

Sincerely yours,

H. L. Mencken

1. Mencken's acquaintance with Clarence Darrow was cemented when he persuaded the celebrated trial lawyer and libertarian to volunteer his ser-

vices to the defense at the Scopes trial in Dayton, Tennessee, in 1925. Darrow wrote occasionally for the *American Mercury*.

[T L S (postscript handwritten)]   Baltimore
                                         April 11th [1927]

Dear Miss Hood:—

We are in the same boat. Every time I dine with the fair I am reported engaged, and sometimes even married. When I got home from the South and West I found a whole drawer full of clippings describing such tender affairs, usually with a large portrait of the lady. Well, they are always very sightly gals, so I don't repine. If any newspaper reporter asks me about my marriage to you, I shall admit it at once, and tell him that I am writing an opera for you.

It is too infernally bad that I can't come to dinner next Sunday, but my niece and her ma will be here.[1] On Saturday I may have to take her to Washington to see the sights. I wonder if you'll be free for lunch. If so, why not meet us at the Madrillon at 12.30. But I'm afraid her chatter will knock you cold. Worse, I'll probably have to see a newspaper woman who is doing an article for The American Mercury.[2] But if Christian charity is in you, you will come.

I am in my usual low state, and scarcely able to work.

Sincerely yours,

H. L. MENCKEN

My brother is recovering[3]

1. Virginia Mencken, of whom her uncle was especially fond, was the daughter of Charles and his wife, Mary; at this time she was eleven.
2. Duff Gilfond, a Washington journalist who wrote several articles on the Congress and its members for the *Mercury*. Her profile of La Guardia appeared in the June 1927 issue. *G.H.*: "We became good friends & she later introduced me to Fiorello La Guardia, then in Congress. After that La G. had me for dinner at his apt. on que St (next to Cairo hotel) almost *every* Sun. He was superb cook."
3. August Mencken.

[T L S]   Baltimore
                                                      April 13th [1927]

Dear Miss Hood:—

God will punish you for having at me with sarcasm. But if you
don't appear at the Madrillon at 12.30 on Saturday I shall send my
dragoman after you. I'll be on the lookout for you.

My niece is also a literary woman. She is at work on a novel, and
hopes to complete it by her 12th birthday.

But is holy matrimony suitable for us artists? I must take the
advice of my pastor on that.

Yours,

H. L. MENCKEN

G.H.: "*Yes, I lunched with him & his niece Virginia—also Duff Gilfond. . . . After our luncheon HLM, Virginia & I went down to see Mt.
Vernon. That was the most hilarious 'education' I ever had. I was determined then to spend the rest of my life with him but alas, knew nothing of
his protegee at Goucher, in Balt. She was in on the ground floor, way back.
He never, in those years, ever spoke her name to me.*"

[T L S (date handwritten)]   Baltimore
                                                      Monday Apr. 18, '27

Dear Miss Hood:—

Hell was loose when I got home. My brother had had a nose
operation last week. Saturday afternoon he had a hemorrhage from
the wound, and Saturday evening, after I got home, two more,
both very severe. At midnight we had to take him back to hospital,
and there he is now. I don't think there will be any more, but he is
pretty well used up.

More when this uproar is over.

Yours,

M

[TLS]   Baltimore
                                             April 20th [1927]

Dear Miss Hood:—

My brother, by dint of prayer, seems to be recovered. Now the
problem is to find out what happened to him, and prevent it
happening again. The surgeons are at the job this afternoon. He is
on his legs, and says he feels very well.

My business with La Gilfond was brief, and we had finished it
when you came in: a discussion of an article she is doing. Her
automobile driving is beautifully wavy. What the country would
have lost if she had ditched us! The thought made me tremble.

The local tabloid called me up an hour ago, and said that it had a
report that I was engaged to a lovely creature in Washington. I told
the reporter that it was possible, but that I had not yet heard of it.
He said he had no name, but I think he lied. Well, let them wait for
March 3rd, 1929.

I am gradually getting back to work. My best thanks for the
cartoon.

                                        Yours in Xt.,[1]

                                             M

G.H.: *"Thus the horrid publicity began. It hounded us. . . . All this
publicity began to upset his protegee, in Balt. I fear (I heard many things
later) and was responsible for the finale. Of that I'm dead sure[.] I was
completely in the dark—never knowing she existed!"*

1. Mencken's humorous use of "Yours in Christ" is of a piece with his occasionally enclosing religious tracts in his letters.

[TLS]   Baltimore
                                             May 6, 1927.

Dear Miss Hood:

I am off for the great wastes of North Carolina.[1] If you hear of
me playing golf down there you have a free license to shoot me at

sight. I expect to devote my whole time to the booze arts. The local brews are terrible, but the intelligentsia import very good Scotches.

The artist who painted me in New York is Nikol Schattenstein. He is a Viennese and very well known in his own country. The red breeches are supposed to be a delicate hint that if I had gone into the church as a young man I'd have been an archbishop by now and close to a red hat.[2]

It never occurred to me that La Gilfond was of the Old Testament but now that you mention it I begin to recall certain indications of it. The Jews are everywhere. It is hopeless to try to avoid them. Worse, they are all damnably clever. She has done better work for Washington than any of the male Washington correspondents that I have tackled. More anon when I return from the wilds.

Yours,

M

1. Around this time, Mencken began to make visits to the summer home of Dr. and Mrs. Frederic M. Hanes in the North Carolina mountains.
2. Schattenstein's portrait, which now hangs in the Mencken Room of the Enoch Pratt Free Library, captures a casually posed Mencken with cigar in hand, rolled-up shirt sleeves, an open collar, and red trousers and suspenders. *G.H.:* "The painting created a stir—a 100% American. Have a framed copy on my wall."

[TLS]   Baltimore
                                          May 14th [1927]

Dear Miss Hood:—

You have the psychoanalytical gift! The secret fact is that I am full of regret that I didn't go into the Church as a young man. I'd have been a bishop by now, as sure as the devil. I have a natural talent for theology, and could train up to a 50 inch waist without much trouble. A bishop is the most enviable man in the world. He gets a drink out of every bottle. More, the gals are not averse to testing the truth of the whispers about him. When he dies he sits upon the right hand of God.

I am putting in a radio to hear you. My first call will be for "Die Wacht am Rhein".[1] You are just in time with your application for "I Am a 100% American". The last 100 is oozing away. I'll have to have it reprinted.

My sister-in-law wires that she is coming down from Pittsburgh for some surgery. I'll try to plant her in a hospital tomorrow, and then duck for New York. Knopf is sailing Monday, to be gone 3 months, and I must see him before he goes.[2] Thus my time is frittered away, and the swell letters of the nation suffers.

Yours,

M

1. "The Watch on the Rhine," a German patriotic song written in 1840, became a national hymn at the time of the Franco-Prussian War.

2. Alfred A. Knopf had been Mencken's publisher since 1916 and was the publisher of the *American Mercury*.

[TLS]   Baltimore
                                        Thursday [May 19, 1927]

Dear Miss Hood:—
That movie article was written before I had enjoyed the felicity of meeting you. I gave it to Jim Quirk as a wedding present: he had just been married to May Allison. Now he has given me an article on the movie censors, and I shall print it in July.[1] A noble Irishman!

My sister-in-law is in for some tedious treatment—an old sinus bust loose. She'll probably be here for several weeks. But I can I can get away for an evening in your great city, if you are kind enough to ask me again, after all these delays. What of Sunday a week?

I bought a car in 1915, ran it and damned it for 3 years, and then sold it to a Jew. Now I use taxicabs, and am getting rich. What you say of my compositions soothes my gills. I ascribe their merit to my life-long use of Father John's medicine.[2] More of this anon.

Last night, in Union Hill, N.J., I discovered the best beer heard of in America since 1917.³ Unfortunately, I reached it at the end of the evening, and so could not get much of it down. But I shall go back.

Yours,

M

1. Mencken's "The Low-Down on Hollywood," in the April issue of *Photoplay*, spoke of fan letters he claimed to have written to movie stars: "Perhaps many a worthy and beautiful girl at Hollywood cherishes such a letter today, wondering all the while how Seth Burkhardt, of Red Lion, Pa., ever achieved so delicate and eloquent a prose style" (32:119). James R. Quirk, the publisher of *Photoplay*, and movie actress May Allison were among Mencken's cohorts during his stay in Hollywood the previous fall; they were married immediately after Mencken's visit. Quirk's article for the *Mercury*, "The Wowsers Tackle the Movies," ridiculed the advocates of public censorship.

2. A popular patent medicine of the day.

3. Union Hill was one of the places Mencken frequented, when in New York, in his continual search for good beer during Prohibition.

[TLS]   Baltimore
                                             May 25th [1927]

Dear Miss Hood:—

God damn it one million times! Again I am stuck! The heavenly hierarchy seems to have me blacklisted. My niece is coming down on Sunday to visit her mother, and so I must stay here. But this persecution can't go on. I have a plan, of which more presently.

You would be fully justified in telling me to go to hell, and refusing to speak to me hereafter.

Yours,

M

G.H.: *"Too bad I didn't take his advice & tell him 'to go to hell'—then & there. It would have spared me much heartache & mental anguish later, not to mention taunts from so-called friends & anonymous letters."*

[TLS]   Baltimore
                                    June 23rd [1927]

Dear Miss Hood:—

Forgotten it! Not on your life! I'm coming back to do it again.
My sister-in-law, after long struggles, seems to be getting better,
and I shall go to New York in a few days and clear up a pile of
accumulated work. Will you be in Washington Sunday a week? If
you say yes, I'll be there then, absolutely without fail. I hope you
let me come.

The 100% American song is free to any 100% American who
wants to sing or publish it. Tell them all to lay on! I enclose a
review of the Siegfried book that I printed in the Nation last
month.[1] Siegfried sent me a letter of thanks. Like all Frogs of
intelligence, he is Hunnish.

Prejudices VI is finished. It is so bad that I am tinkering with it,
and hope to make it worse. Now for a dozen or two long-delayed
small jobs, including a Selected Prejudices for Germany and
Sweden.

I haven't seen the Bodenheim piece.[2] He is a poor fish.

                                    Yours,

                                    M

1. Mencken lauded André Siegfried's *America Comes of Age: A French View*
   as "the most accurate, penetrating, and comprehensive treatise on the
   United States ever written, whether by a native or a foreigner." He was
   particularly taken with the French scholar's view that at the heart of present-day America lay the conflict between the native Anglo-Saxon Protestant populace and the heterogeneous newer Americans. This contention
   accorded with Mencken's own persistent antipathy toward the Anglo-
   philic hegemony in American politics, literature, and culture. ("A
   Frenchman Takes a Look," *Nation*, 11 May 1927, pp. 533–34.)

2. Presumably, Bodenheim's letter in the *New York World* (June 19) protesting Mencken's column on how writers should approach editors. After
   Hood's answer to Bodenheim appeared, Mencken wrote to her on June
   29: "He [God] will reward you for that *World* letter. The righteous store
   up treasures in Heaven."

[TLS]   Baltimore
                                                   July 1st [1927]

Dear Miss Hood:—

Under God's hand I shall arrive in your great city at 4.15 on
Sunday, and come direct to your house. Put me down for 20
bottles of beer, and a couple of slugs of White Horse. You don't
mention Moselle. I shall bring you a bottle of it, for the next dinner
you give to my hero, Dawes.[1] He is a charter member of the
enclosed association.[2] I shall devote all of my time in July to
furthering its cause.

As for La Gilfond and her consort, I leave it to you. Why should
I yearn for literary negotiations when I have you to talk to? The
answer baffles me.

                                                   Yours,

                                                   M

1. Charles G. Dawes, Vice-President of the United States, 1924–28. To
   Mencken, he epitomized business-minded America: "His ethical ideas are
   simple and devoid of cant. He believes that any man deserves whatever he
   can get. This is also the notion of at least 98 per cent of his countrymen."
   ("Autopsy," *Baltimore Evening Sun* Monday article, 10 Nov. 1924.)
2. Mencken enclosed several copies of his flyer for the "Tobacco-Chewers'
   Protective and Educational League of America," purporting that Henrik
   Ibsen was a secret chewer. (In Mencken/Hood Collection.)

[TLS]   Baltimore
                                                   July 4th [1927]

Dear Gretchen:—

It was a noble evening! What a programme: scotch, cocktails,
sauterne, Burgundy, two liqueurs, and beer! I feel like a genuine
artist. Please give your mother my very best thanks. As for you, I
kiss your hand. It was immensely pleasant to hear of old John
Burkhardt, one of my heroes as a boy.[1] And old John McCarthy,
who started me as a stamp collector at six![2]

Aren"t you ever going to New York? Why not make it soon, and
let me lead you into my cellar? All the saloon-keepers know me,

and, I trust, respect me. Caplan's new drinking-room is really superb—a sort of beer cathedral.

Mid the rockets' red glare I salute you!

Yours,

M

G.H.: *"Here he begins to call me by my first name. . . . He 'took to' mom at once—she* was *bonnie & full of the joy of living and we served him a fine dinner—at least, I thought so."*

1. John Burkhardt had run a saloon that Mencken fondly remembered as the best in Washington in his youth.
2. Evidently, another old Washingtonian—possibly John B. McCarthy, a contemporary of Edwin Hood in the Washington press corps.

[T L S]
Baltimore
June 8th [July 8, 1927]

Dear Gretchen:—

I'll be in New York off and on all through August and September. If hay-fever toys with me it won't matter: it is always possible to relieve it with ethyl alcohol, administered in large doses per ora. I am taking a vaccine again, but have no belief in it. But a war-hero has duties to his country.

On July 29th I am going down into North Carolina, and from there I must go to St. Louis, where a libel suit threatens.[1] In the meanwhile I must make a trip or two to New York. So I may not be able to come to Washington during the next few weeks. But if the chance turns up I'll certainly seize the first express. That was a superb dinner!

My sister-in-law is to go home on Sunday. She has been here nearly eight weeks.

Yours,

M

The sheath will and must be found!

G.H.: *"Alas! the 'sheath' never was found!! Perhaps that was my mistake. At the time he wrote that, I was so green, so naive, I had no inkling of what he meant. . . . Only after I'd read 'Jurgen' a bit later did I get the drift! I recall in N. Y. he asked me if I was 'still a virgin' & I replied: 'Not yet.' I still can see the look of complete bafflement on his face & only then did I reveal that I'd been married way back in 1914, but left the clod I'd wed, after only one month and ten days together, never to see him again."*

Mencken alludes to the following passage in James Branch Cabell's *Jurgen* (Storisende Ed., VI, New York: R. M. McBride [1928], pp. 120–21):

So Jurgen put his arm about the ghost of Queen Sylvia Tereu, and comforted her. Then, finding her quite willing to be comforted, Jurgen sat for a while upon the dark steps, with one arm still about Queen Sylvia. The effect of the potion had evidently worn off, because Jurgen found himself to be composed no longer of cool imponderable vapor, but of the warmest and hardest sort of flesh everywhere. But probably the effect of the wine which Jurgen had drunk earlier in the evening had not worn off: for now Jurgen began to talk wildishly in the dark, about the necessity of his, in some way, avenging the injury inflicted upon his nominal grandfather, Ludwig, and Jurgen drew his sword, charmed Caliburn.

"For, as you perceive," said Jurgen, "I carry such weapons as are sufficient for all ordinary encounters. And am I not to use them, to requite King Smoit for the injustice he did poor Ludwig? Why, certainly I must. It is my duty."

"Ah, but Smoit by this hour is back in Purgatory," Queen Sylvia protested. "And to draw your sword against a woman is cowardly."

"The avenging sword of Jurgen, my charming Sylvia, is the terror of envious men, but it is the comfort of all pretty women."

"It is undoubtedly a very large sword," said she: "oh, a magnificent sword, as I can perceive even in the dark. But Smoit, I repeat, is not here to measure weapons with you."

"Now your arguments irritate me, whereas an honest woman would see to it that all the legacies of her dead husband were duly satisfied—"

"Oh, oh! and what do you mean—?"

"Well, but certainly a grandson is—at one remove, I grant you,—a sort of legacy."

"There is something in what you advance—"

"There is a great deal in what I advance, I can assure you. It is the most natural and most penetrating kind of logic; and I wish merely to discharge a duty—"

"But you upset me, with that big sword of yours, you make me nervous, and I cannot argue so long as you are flourishing it about. Come now, put up your sword! Oh, what is anybody to do with you! Here is the sheath for your sword," says she.

At this point they were interrupted.

---

1. The *American Mercury* was threatened with a suit by the owner of the Becky Thatcher–Tom Sawyer cave in Hannibal, Missouri, because an article in the magazine had asserted that the popular tourist stop was unsafe to explore.

[T L S]   Baltimore
                                           July 13th [1927]

Dear Gretchen:—

If you can get me out of the Ulman dinner party I'll pray for you in Hell. I said yes because your velvet tones were in my ear, but I hate all dinner parties where strangers are to be met. Consider my advanced years! And when God in His infinite mercy lets me get to Washington I want to see you. It is seldom enough.

Poor Bodenheim! He has a dreadful failure complex. He was spoiled by excessive praise in his early days, chiefly done by Louis Untermeyer,[1] and probably with tongue in cheek. Now he is simply a poor fish, fighting off oblivion.

I must go to New York Sunday, probably to stay all week. I hope to be able to visit your great city the week following. But if not, then certainly we meet in August in the celebrated city of New

York. I'll give you a party in my cellar, which is under the sidewalk of Fifth ave at 56th street.

Temperature here: 100 degrees. What a world!

Yours,

M

G.H.: *"Bodenheim began bombarding me with deadly boring letters special delivery which roused me at all hours after midnight. . . . I'd seen him many times in Greenwich Village when I wrote for the Greenwich Villager. . . . I never met Bodenheim while I lived there. Everyone said he was too argumentative, boring & fawning & was disliked by most every one. His letters prove those points."*

1. Poet, critic, and anthologist, who championed many of the new poets in the teens and early twenties.

[T L S (postscript handwritten)]   Baltimore
                                      July 15th [1927]

Dear Gretchen:—

My profound apologies. I thought the party was just a dinner party. Certainly I want to hear you sing—in fact, I shall have at you with a complete programme. More of this anon, when I find out what I'll be up against when I get back from New York. I am even contemplating writing a song for you.[1]

I have just been reading "The President's Daughter", by Nan Britton, who alleges that Harding was the father of her child. The Comstocks tried to suppress the book, but failed. It is surely not indecent. But Nan tells the old sad, mad, glad story very effectively.[2]

When will you be in New York? I get news today that there is no more beer in New Jersey. But I have heard such tales before. They are spread by Christians in order to worry me. Courage!

Yours,

M

All your moody thoughts are nonsense.

1. Hood does not mention whether Mencken came to the Ulman dinner party, but she notes that on July 23 they lunched at the Mayflower Hotel in Washington, "where many of my pals were dining & all flocked to our table to meet such a celebrity. Am sure, many had doubted that I knew *The Man*. Such are friends! Later, we walked all around down town, I answering his dozens of questions."

2. In his July 18 column in the *Evening Sun,* titled "Saturnalia," Mencken called attention to Britton's book and its publishing history to introduce his own dissection of Harding's presidency: "What makes the Britton story engrossing is not the tale of good Warren's mushy love-making, but the picture of him as statesman that emerges from the fair penitent's pages. Miss Britton is naive, but by no means ignorant: her writing is extremely vivid. What she achieves is a portrait so grotesque that it seems fabulous, and yet so palpably true that it convinces instantly."

   After the New York Society for the Suppression of Vice failed to prevent publication, the book gained underground notoriety, but was generally ignored by reviewers. Mencken's column ended the silence.

[TLS]   Baltimore
                                         July 29th [1927]

Dear Gretchen:—

Quit your blarney, woman! You will make me swell up like a movie actor. Remember the sad fate of Valentino![1]

I enclose a still of the Baltimore champion.[2] He mastered the art playing on an excursion-boat in Chesapeake Bay. True enough, he can't read notes, but he is a wonder doing it by ear.

As soon as I find out when I'll be able to get to New York I'll write to you. It will probably be on August 9th, but possible it won't be until August 14th. I am confronted by a mass of necessary writing, and I don't think I'll be able to do any of it on the train. In any case I'll be in New York more than once before September 1st.

Ich kuss die Hand.

                                         Yours,

                                         M

1. Mencken concluded *Prejudices: Sixth Series,* then in press, with an essay on Rudolph Valentino. It recounts an interview between the two men in July 1926—a month before the film star's death. Valentino asked Mencken's advice about how to deal with the ridicule he was exposed to by the press

after he challenged an editorial writer to a fight for impugning his mas-
culine honor. The sketch sympathetically portrays Valentino as suffering
"the agony of a man of relatively civilized feelings thrown into a situation
of intolerable vulgarity"—an unhappiness that, in turn, reflected his deeper recognition of the "grotesque futility" of his "vast and dizzy success."

2. Photograph of Mencken. *G.H.:* "HLM, seated at piano, back to camera,
in undershirt & suspenders, pounding away. Inscribed to me: 'As one
artist to another.'"

[TLS]   Baltimore
                                        August 8th [1927]

Dear Gretchen:—

I'll surely be in the next car, and shall look you up as soon as we
get under way. Maybe it will be possible to transfer to a drawing
room, and so have lunch there, and get a chance at a jug of van
rouge.[1] If my sister gets car-sick it will give her a chance to lie
down, and so recover. I'll put her in a taxicab at the Pennsylvania
Station in New York. If you are going to Madison avenue I'll drop
you there. If you can't have dinner with me tomorrow night, what
of lunch on Wednesday? My cellar at the Algonquin Palace Hotel is
rich in all the noblest essences of the grape and malt-bush.

The New York *News* called me up too. I said I was flattered, but
labored under an oath to preserve my chastity. All the Maryland
fortune tellers say that I'll end in a monastery. What do you make
of that?

                                        Yours,

                                        M

G.H.: "*Yes, we travelled together, with his sister Gertrude—had a
room & meals together. . . . Had dinner same eve at Algonquin. Later
went out, visited the beer palaces etc.*"

1. *Vin rouge.*

[ALS]   New York
                                             [August 11, 1927]

Dear Gretchen:

Edwards proposes that I pose for him in the altogether.[1] But
this, I fear, would only unsettle the minds of thousands of worthy
girls. I shall insist upon boxing trunks, at least.

You were an angel to be polite to those Saccos![2] As you are
always.

                              Yours,

                              M

This letter and the four which follow were sent to various addresses where Hood stayed in New York City.

1. Bobby Edwards, Hood's friend and former editor of *The Quill*, was a
   photographer.
2. A couple from Italy who lunched with Hood and Mencken in his Algonquin suite. Nicola Sacco, whose name Mencken employs here, and Bar-
   tolomeo Vanzetti were to be executed on August 23.

[TLS]   Baltimore
                                             Sunday [August 14, 1927]

Dear Gretchen:—

I have been grinding away all day at the index to Prejudices VI—
a dreadful chore, but now happily done by God's assistance. The
house is empty. My sister and brother are away, and the refined
Moorish lady, Mrs. Zorah Savoy—that is her actual name!—
vanished after making my bed, emptying my waste-basket, and
putting the week's wash in soak. I lunched on three plates of capital
crab-soup at a bootlegger's nearby. Such is the literary life!

You generalize too boldly from your own experience. Look in
the glass! How often do they see such a gal? Not once in a blue
moon. The Pope himself would begin to wobble. But in general

the American husband is an honest and worthy fellow. I shall continue to defend him.

The hay-fever vaccines are powerful stuff, and have got me half groggy. The disease itself is not half so bad. But my curse is conscientiousness. I can't get rid of the idea that I ought to let the pathological boys have some fun with me now and then, and so give the poor guinea pigs a rest.

I kiss both your hands!

Yours,

M

[T L S]   Baltimore
                                                 Friday [August 19, 1927]

Dear Gretchen:—

The professors gave me another dreadful dose of vaccine today, and I am quite useless tonight. In an hour I hope to go out to Catonsville and land in a beer party. No women allowed! It is for sturdy drinkers only, and dogs are sent out at dawn to rescue any that have got lost in the woods. Tomorrow I proceed to Hergesheimer's palace at West Chester, to cool off.[1] He is on the water-wagon, and we shall put in two days discussing the Sacco-Vanzetti case and other high matters.[2] I shall take along a bottle of Erdner Treppchen, and drink it myself.

I promise to tell you that Long Island story within ten days after March 4, 1928, in the Blue Room. It is an appalling saga of high society. I rolled down a sand-dune 800 feet high.[3]

A deadly dull day, slaving away at MSS. and struggling with mail. My stenographer will soon pass away, the ninth I have killed in eight years. I always bury them with full Masonic honors.

I kiss both your hands.

Yours,

M

1. Mencken often weekended at the Pennsylvania home of novelist Joseph Hergesheimer and his wife, Dorothy.

2. The appeals and protests on behalf of the two anarchists were now at
their height. Despite his flippant tone here, Mencken had earlier contributed to the Sacco-Vanzetti defense fund; reviewing their original trial in
his Monday article for August 15, 1927, he called it "a complete burlesque
of the judicial process."

3. Two days before, Mencken had written Hood, who was visiting there:
"Long Island is dreadful. I once spent a week-end there at the house of
my old partner, Warner, and—but the story would only horrify you. Alcohol, as you know, is lighter than water. When I fell overboard I floated
like a bladder."

Eltinge F. Warner became the publisher of the *Smart Set* in 1914 and
installed Mencken and George Jean Nathan as co-editors. The three
jointly operated the magazine until 1923.

[TLS]   Baltimore
                                  August 24th [1927]

Dear Gretchen:—

I am very eager to hear what you encountered at the Woman
Pays Club.[1] Some of them are awful harridans, but there are also
some amusing women, who don't take the Lucy Stone nonsense
seriously. Even most of the Lucy Stoners have a good excuse: look
at their husbands.

There is a high wind here today, and in consequence it is perfect
hay-fever weather. But so far I have done no snuffling. The malaise,
however, is on me, and all this afternoon I have been snoozing and
unable to work. Meanwhile, the work undone piles up mountain-
high. I got a dreadful shot of vaccine yesterday—enough to knock
off a Sacco.

Do we meet on Tuesday?

                                        Yours,

                                          M

1. A Menckenism. While in New York, Hood evidently attended a meeting
of the Lucy Stone League; founded by Ruth Hale, the wife of Heywood
Broun, and named for a nineteenth-century feminist, the League sought
to win the legal right for a married woman to retain her maiden name.
Writing again, on August 25, Mencken commented: "The Wronged Gals
of that club really deserve an article. One of them, I hear, has made three

melodramatic (and faked) attempts at suicide. Many of the rest are great sufferers from female weakness. It is a wicked world."

[TLS]   Baltimore
                                                     September 7th [1927]

Dear Gretchen:—

Excellent! I'll look for you at the Algonquin Palace Hotel at 6.15 on Wednesday. I suggest that we dine there, and then maybe go to the Paramount and see Hanke, if he is free.[1] Or to some quiet beer-saloon.

I fear you won't know me. I have aged immensely, and am now definitely an aged man. The hay-fever Sunday was so bad that my hair turned gray overnight. The plain fact is that I have passed midlife and am now sliding downhill toward the fires. Well, I was a gay dog in my day! So was Andy Mellon in his.[2]

I feel much better, and am getting some work done. Nothing has been heard from Knopf, but I assume that he will have landed by the time I get to N.Y.

Your hand is kissed!

                                                     Yours,

                                                     M

1. The Paramount movie theater on Times Square. Hanke is not identified.
2. Andrew Mellon, Pittsburgh financier and Secretary of the Treasury under Harding, Coolidge, and Hoover, was generally regarded as an exemplar of conservative reserve and respectability.

[TLS]   Baltimore
                                                     September 18th [1927]

Dear Gretchen:—

Don't let those tabloid boys worry you! I think I have shut them off. But my heart ain't in it: the business flatters me. I told them that they were up the wrong alley: that you were engaged to a man worth $40,000. The next time I shall mention Ronald [Colman].[1]

The fault is all mine. Some indiscretions in Atlanta last
November set off the story that I was about to be married, and it
has been going about ever since.[2] I am sorry indeed that you are its
victim now. But you deserve it for being so nice to the oldest man
in America.

I am still uncomfortable, mainly because of the infernal heat. A
cool day or two would cure me. It is dreadfully hard to work in
such weather. I melt into the Corona.

I hope you let me come to see you soon.

Yours,

M

G.H.: *"Here it really starts in earnest: my life was made miserable—
phone calls, letters, spite mail (anonymous of course) & the whole town
buzzing. Am sure it had something to do with my failure. He thought I
was angry. It wasn't that—I really hoped to marry him, based on things
he said; but I was angry at the way it was handled & such publicity
breaking without consulting either of us. And I was afraid he was angry.
What a mess!*

*"He probably was, now that I realize, years later, that his 'protegee'
couldn't take it. She* must *have read the papers. It probably aggravated
her illness. And I knew nothing of woe I caused her!"*

1. Then enjoying his early film success as a romantic leading man.
2. Stories linking Mencken and Frances Newman, an Atlanta journalist and
   novelist whose literary career he had personally encouraged, appeared
   after he visited the city in October 1926—not November.

[TLS]   Baltimore
                                   September 19th [1927]

Dear Gretchen:—

I am sorry indeed that I brought down those Hearst vermin
upon you. What journalism has come to in their hands! Please tell
your mother how sorry I am. But there seems to be no way to stop

them. Since last November they have reported me married six times. Why such stuff should be printed I don't know. It is a wonder they didn't accuse you of poisoning me! I was visibly wobbly.

The cool weather today has relieved me, and I begin to feel alive again. I must have been a ghastly object on the train.[1]

Ich kuss die Hand.

Yours,

M

1. After dining together the previous evening, Mencken and Hood had returned from New York by train on September 15.

[TLS]   Baltimore
                                        September 24th [1927]

Dear Gretchen:—

I am rocky, out of sorts, and in no mood for work—no doubt all sequelae of catarrhus aestivus.[1] But all that will pass very soon. My pastor's prayers seem to be less effective than they used to be, when sound beer was on tap everywhere in Baltimore at 5 cents a glass. The present needle beer is too expensive for a clergyman.[2] And his wife's home brew is as bad as her complexion.

So far as I know, the Hearst papers here printed nothing about our elopment to Elkton. A few Baltimoreans linger on their staffs. I have seen no clippings save the one from the rag in Washington.[3] No doubt more will come in the coming week: the clippings burueaus are often slow.

Let me hear of it a day ahead when you come this way, so that I can clear my decks. You are elected to devour lunch with me at the Marconi kaffy.[4]

Yours,

M

1. "Aftereffects of the summer catarrh." *G.H.:* "Was ever a man so beset by physical ailments? I wonder if he realized how he dwelt on them? Most people don't, who are hypocondrias like him. Nothing was ever that bad!

If I'd married him, would such obscessions have held him? Maybe I would have been the cure! He lost out."

2. Needle beer, an ersatz beer made with ether alcohol, was popular during Prohibition. Mencken wrote of the term in *The American Language:* "*Near-beer* appeared in 1920, but did not last long. It continued to be brewed, but before it reached the consumer it was usually converted into *needle-beer*" (*Supplement I* [New York: Alfred A. Knopf, 1945], p. 264n).

3. *Washington Times,* Sept. 17. Another story appeared on the same date in the *New York Daily Mirror.* (Clippings in Mencken/Hood Collection.)

4. They lunched together at the Baltimore restaurant on September 28. *G.H.:* "Went to Balt. to the Marconi & feasted fabulously. All it was 'cracked up' to be & then some. Strange, not a soul bothered us there, after all that hoo-haw in the papers."

[TLS]
Baltimore
Friday [September 30, 1927]

Dear Gretchen:—

Thanks very much for the page from the Star. I found two superb gems in it, and shall print them, along with others, in an early issue of our great moral journal.[1] My stuff is printed in the Evening Sun on Mondays. I'll send it to you whenever I am here, but sometimes I am not, and so don't see it myself. On the coming Monday I'll either be in New York, or on my way.

This infernal weather is gradually killing me. And I seem to be surrounded by embalmers. Tomorrow I am to be a pallbearer for an old lady next door, and now I hear that one of my aunts has just passed to God's arms. Such things run by threes. Maybe Elinor Glyn will be next.[2]

I was afraid your mother had put me on her black list on account of that Hearst stuff. Tell her I damned them enough, but it did no good.

Ich kuss die Hand.

Yours,

M

1. *Washington Evening Star.* Mencken was culling quotations for the *Mercury*'s "Americana" section, which held up contemporary national life to

ridicule by displaying fatuous or absurd excerpts from various sources. The following entry appeared in the January 1928 issue (p. 50):

> PEARLS of wisdom from the gifted editorial writers of the Washington *Star:*
>
> Easy and accessible forms of communications are always harbingers of better understanding and good will. . . .
> The personal element in negotiations, no matter how involved, has its place. . . .
> Thoughtfulness is an attribute that should be assiduously cultivated. . . .
> Every man and every woman should have a full sense of responsibility, not only to those about him, but to the community as well. . . .
> No one can go his own way through life willy nilly, looking neither right nor left. . . .

2. An English writer of highly popular romantic fiction, Glyn worked in Hollywood between 1920 and 1927, writing film scenarios and columns for the Hearst papers, and became the film capital's resident authority on love.

[TLS]   Baltimore
                                             October 1st [1927]

Dear Gretchen:—

I have been to a funeral today and must go to another tomorrow. What I object to is the obscene way in which the undertakers look at me and rub their hands. Certainly I must hold out until 1932. Then for a bronze casket, and a salute of 21 guns! You are to wear no veil!

Ritchie is probably beginning to get skeered—his old fault. If he had more bellicosity he would get further. But I observe that even Jim Reed is beginning to hedge. What a gang!

Hal Smith I don't know. But I knew old Louis Garthe.[1] He wrote, in his day, 25,000 columns of sound Republican doctrine. If you take Eaton's shilling, let me know.[2] We can pose for some movies.

I am half dead of the heat. It is very hard on a man of my years. Taft goes to Canada, but I am stuck here.[3]

Yours,

M

1. Smith is probably Hal Harrison Smith, a veteran Washington reporter for the *New York Times*. Garthe was the late Washington correspondent for the *Baltimore American*.

2. G. D. Eaton, formerly literary editor of the *New York Telegraph*, had just brought out the first issue of *Plain Talk*, a magazine closely modeled on the *American Mercury*. Hood had become friendly with him through Duff Gilfond. *G.H.:* "I've a faint recollection Geff Eaton asked me to contribute to his mag."

3. Chief Justice William Howard Taft had recently celebrated his seventieth birthday at his summer home in Quebec.

[TLS]   New York
                                         October 5. [1927]

Dear Gretchen:

My Chicago *Tribune* article is printed in the *Evening Sun* on Saturdays—that is usually. Sometimes, when it discusses a subject that I have already covered in my Monday article, it is omitted. It is seldom worth reading. I knock it off simply in order to procure money for my contributions to foreign missions.

I didn't see the World's editorial on Al Smith[1] and I shall certainly not attend the debate between Bertrand Russell and Will Durant.[2] Russell is not bad, but Durant is rather a nuisance.

I am gradually returning to normalcy and hope to resume work in the grand manner when I get back to Baltimore. Enough of it is accumulated to keep me jumping for six months. The Summer was very unfavorable to sustained intellectual activity. First it was too cold and then it was infernally hot. I ascribe all this to the personal animosity of God.

What is your judgment as a political expert? Shall I announce my candidacy at once or wait until Al Smith is disposed of by the Klu Klux? Please don't forget that I am a Democrat, not a Republican. To be sure, I always vote the Republican ticket, but I have been on the books as a Democrat of Maryland since the second Grant campaign.

Yours,

M

1. On September 30, the *New York World* called on Smith to make himself known on national issues to the country at large, if his presidential candidacy was to mean "a rebirth of a high liberalism within the Democratic Party" ("The Unknown Al Smith," p. 12).

2. The British philosopher and the American historian of philosophy debated the question "Is Democracy a Failure?" in New York on October 23.

[TLS] Baltimore
Friday [October 7, 1927]

Dear Gretchen:—

The best way to have at the Albany Silurian would be by magic.[1] This town swarms with sorcerers. Say the word and I'll slip one of them a $10 bill. It will not be necessary to give his name. Simply find the date of his birth, and let me know when he was baptized, and by what rite. If it was the Latin rite there will be difficulties about the Holy Saints. But necromancy can fetch them. Then for the South Seas!

I am trying to knock off some delayed writing, but find it hard. My old lovely fluency is gone. I grow so senile that I have to think before writing. I'll go to New York Sunday morning, but shall be back by Monday night. Unfortunately, the evening will be wasted, for there is to be a big banquet to Black given by the Baltimore Babbitts, and I want to see it.[2] Luckily, I know very few of them. But the speeches will be instructive.

God help us one and all! I begin to fear that another war is brewing.[3] Well, if it comes I shall leap out heroically again. We heroes never get enough!

Ich kuss die Hand!

Yours,

M

1. *G.H.*: "'Albany Silurian' means nothing to me now—can't recall except that a cousin of my dad's . . . living there died & named me in his will."

2. Van-Lear Black, Baltimore financier and chairman of the board of the *Sunpapers,* was being honored on his return from Europe. While abroad, Black flew in his personal airplane from Glasgow to the Dutch East Indies and then back to Amsterdam—a pioneering feat of long-distance air travel.

3. *G.H.:* "Here is Mencken's first hint of the World War II to come—he talked of it many times."

[T L S]   Baltimore
                                              October 11th [1927]

Dear Gretchen:—

I have put in two lovely and inspiring days. Sunday I went to New York with the Black committee, and sat through a dull dinner. Monday morning I dropped into the office, and found that Herman Scheffauer, my German agent, had committed suicide.[1] Yesterday I came down with the gang in a special car, and last night I sat through the longest and worst banquet ever heard of. Tonight I must go to a dance in honor of the two Dutch pilots.[2] What a life! John Smith, mayor of Detroit, is due here Thursday. Five or six other visitors are in the offing. Saturday I must entertain the music club. Sunday is a Maryland Free State affair.[3] And my desk is piled mountain high.

The Scheffauer business was dreadful. The poor fellow went crazy, murdered his secretary with a butcher-knife, and then stood at an open window, hacked his throat in the presence of a crowd, and jumped out. His eccentricities of late had put me to a lot of trouble. Now, I suppose, the translation of "Notes on Democracy" will go forward. The old rule holds: anyone who bothers me perishes. Tell the man who alleges that I am crazy to beware. Let Horace J. Donnelly see his pastor.[4]

I am in favor of immediate war with Mexico.[5] The United States at war is a superb show. I love heroes.

If you order Prejudices VI God will punish you. You will get the first copy that comes in. It is due in a few days. As usual, the book is a flawless masterpiece. Try to imagine even Shakespeare writing such stuff! It would have strained Plato.

Last night, at the banquet, I met no less than five candidates for the Presidency. All of them will come to grief.

Your lovely paws are kissed.

Yours,

M

1. An American who had lived and worked as a writer and translator in Germany since 1914, Scheffauer promoted translations of Mencken's books and his publication in German magazines during the twenties.

2. Gerrit J. Geysendorffer and Johann B. Scholte had piloted Van-Lear Black's plane, the *Maryland Free State*.

3. The Maryland Free State Association, an informal group composed of Mencken and several Baltimore friends, periodically hosted dinners, frequently to honor some dignitary visiting the city.

4. As solicitor to the Postmaster-General, Donnelly had banned from the mails the April 1926 issue of the *Mercury,* containing the story "Hatrack." Mencken's chief antagonist in that controversy, J. Franklin Chase, Secretary of the New England Watch and Ward Society, had died suddenly a few months later.

5. In the midst of the Mexican presidential campaign, the Mexican government was currently crushing a military revolt against the regime of President Plutarco Calles and the candidacy of former president Alvaro Obregon.

[T L S]   Baltimore
                                     October 13th [1927]

Dear Gretchen:—

I continue to be surrounded by reminders of mortality. Haslup Adams, chief editor of The Sun, died this morning, and I have spent the afternoon writing an editorial and an article on him for the morning edition.[1] I knew him 27 years. For 12 years he had been crippled by arthritis. This morning his heart failed.

My house is full of painters, and smells like a linseed mill. They will depart, if God so wills, tomorrow. Then follow paperhangers—and the ancient shack is good for 20 more years. I shall retire to it after my second term in 1936. We can pasture little Otto[2] in the backyard, among the turtles. I hope he turns out better than young Teddy Roosevelt.

I have been feeling like hell all week. My senility is bothering me again. But today I feel much better, and hope to work like a horse tomorrow.

Ich kuss die Hand.

                                     Yours,

                                     M

1. John Haslup Adams became managing editor and Mencken associate editor of the newly established *Evening Sun* in 1910. A rift developed between the two men during and immediately after World War I, when Mencken angered the staunchly pro-Wilsonian Adams by his attacks on the President and his policies. They continued as colleagues after 1920, with Adams now editor-in-chief of the morning *Sun*.

2. *G.H.:* "*My* suggestion for naming our first-born—told him 'we could spell it backwards or forwards, drunk or sober.'"

[T L S]   Baltimore
                                                       October 14th [1927]

Dear Gretchen:—

Poor Bodenheim! The notion that there has been "open warfare" between him and me for years is really amusing. I recall mentioning him only a few times, and then to laugh at him. He used to send me verse and beg me to print it. Somewhere in my office files are his letters. Such poor jackasses swarm in the Village. It is full of their lonely graves.

I am pallbearing again tomorrow morning. It begins to be a habit. The dead man, for a change, was a decent fellow. You will need $2,000,000 before we can start our Washington paper. It will cost $500,000 the first year to defend libel suits brought by Washington correspondents.

I am seized with an idea for a string quartette. But don't be alarmed: I'll never write it.

Yours,

M

[T L S]   Baltimore
                                                       October 17th [1927]

Dear Gretchen:—

Saturday night in Hell must have been a terrible one for Brahms. We played his second sextette at the above palace.[1] What music! But I was dam nigh swooning when we finished. No doubt the neighbors will send in another tip that I have a still in my house. Later we drank three cases of beer. Brahms always lifts me tremendously, especially his chamber music. His first trio starts off with the noblest tune ever written.

I could hear you singing "Rule Brittania" even here. But in the White House you'll have to learn "Die Wacht am Rhein". By that time there will be another war, and the Press Bureau will be whooping up German idealism.

I am so badgered by all sorts of petty things that I can't get to work. I had to pass up my Editorial for the December number: it persisted in being bilge.[2] But I surely have a right to drop out now and then.

My engagement to A.P. is off.[3] Her husband made pedantic objections to it. Who started the story, God knows—probably some Hearst reporter. It sprang up about a year ago, and ran along for six months. I had thought it finished at last.

I have not yet seen the Broun article.[4] I'll get it and read it prayerfully.

And kiss your hand.

Yours,

M

1. 1524 Hollins Street.
2. Mencken regularly wrote the editorial and the book reviews for "The Library" in the *American Mercury*.
3. *G.H.:* "The A.P. referred to here was Aileen Pringle, very 'high-brow' movie queen he was fond of too & before he met me."
4. Having temporarily left the *New York World,* Heywood Broun was currently writing a weekly column for the *Nation*. Hood may have called Mencken's attention to the one in the October 5 issue, a tongue-in-cheek assessment of the literary merits of Nan Britton's *The President's Daughter,* or to the one in the October 12 issue, a defense of drinking Mencken would have enjoyed. Possibly, however, if the magazine appeared a few days in advance of the masthead date, Hood may have seen Broun's column in the October 19 number, in which he took issue with Mencken's estimation of the artistic achievements of black Americans.

[TLS]   Baltimore
                                             October 19th [1927]

Dear Gretchen:—

I begin to have bad dreams about Jim Reed: he has been giving
out statements to the effect that Prohibition is not an issue. Thus
they sink, one by one. But they open the way for the Only Honest
Candidate in 1932.

I am banging my way through a pile of accumulated work, and
shall probably go to New York on Sunday. I find that I already
have 17 engagements there, mainly with foreign visitors. They seem
to be swarming this year. In the present bunch are two Swedes and
a Norwegian. They come in, ask for the low-down, and then go
home and publish articles saying that Alfred Kreymborg is a great
poet.[1]

The handsome Aileen, alas, is not rich. She is a poor working
girl, and the Jews keep her jumping. Most of the money in
Hollywood is imaginary.

Ich kuss die Hand.

                                             Yours,

                                             M

1. An early proponent of free verse.

[TLS]   Baltimore
                                             October 22nd [1927]

Dear Gretchen:—

I begin to believe that it will be a shade too easy in 1932—that is,
too easy for a war hero. All the current candidates seem to be
pussyfooting. The effect of a blast of hard, plain language, in 1931,
will be colossal. I have a new idea: you must come on the ticket as
vice-president. Imagine the sensation! Then let us be indissolubly
bound by the Christian rite in front of the capital at noon on
March 4, 1932, to the applause of the whole civilized world.[1] It will

be the greatest story since the Bolsheviki murdered Abraham Lincoln. I trust you to keep your lovely complexion intact until then. Meanwhile, I am applying for membership in the American Legion, Elks, Kiwania and Shrine. You must join the League of American Penwomen.[2]

I am off for New York, where wickedness flourishes. But the office has made 21 engagements for me, and so I expect to lead a righteous life. However, if I don't get my snout into some sound malt it will be a great surprise to me.

Ich kuss die Hand.

Yours,

M

1. Mencken has again confused the inaugural date, which would be 1933.
2. The National League of American Pen Women was founded in 1897 to promote the cultural arts.

[TLS]   New York
                                     October 27th. [1927]

Dear Gretchen:

I come out of a tailspin to send you Christian greetings. This week has been a bull roar and I am getting on my legs just in time to take the swift, expensive express back to the Free State.

As for the advent of March 4, 1932, I put it wholly into your hands. You know Washington better than I do and understand clearly what is proper in the town. All I ask is twenty-four hours notice that I may get a suitable haircut and write a farewell letter to a beautiful movie queen.

More when I get back to base.

Yours,

M

[TLS]   Baltimore
                                         October 29th [1927]

Dear Gretchen:—
   God will punish you throughout Eternity for not giving me
notice of your trip to Baltimore. I had a lunch engagement, but
could have put it off if I had known of your trip an hour or two
earlier. As it was, I was stuck, and had to go through with a very
dull show. You will not suspect me of flattery when I tell you that
lunching with you, even with La Gilfond on the scene, would have
been 1,000, 000, 000, 000, 000, 000, 000, 000, 000 more betterer.
   That damned hay-fever has left me with the usual hacking
morning cough. It is not serious, but it annoys me. It is gone by 10
A.M. The human frame is a dreadful proof of God's incompetence,
malignancy and imbecility. I could design a better one myself, and
half tight.
   The Longworth party sounds superb.[1] Notify me of the time,
and I'll invite myself. All I ask is a chance to sing a duet with you,
in the ancient Sunday-school manner. I suggest "Aunt Dinah's
Quilting Party". Or "Oh, That We Two Were Maying"
   I am off for New York by sleeper tonight, but only for a day. I'll
be back in the mines by Monday.
   And now kiss your hand 260 times.

                              Yours,

                               M

1. Hood's friend Lucille McArthur, a secretary to Nicholas Longworth, had
   proposed the party to the Speaker, who wrote in reply: "I entirely ap-
   prove your suggested symposium. Music and iconoclastic philosophy
   have always been to me most appealing, not to mention cracked ice."
   Hood sent Mencken Longworth's letter, dated October 20, 1927, adding a
   comment of her own: "Here is a letter from Nick Longworth touching
   on the matter of our 'get-together' after his return. I imagine you two
   would have a rare evening in the same room! I'm all for it!" (Letter in
   Mencken/Hood Collection.)

[TLS]

Baltimore
October 29th [1927][1]

Dear Gretchen:—

Your musical skill and cunning will not go to waste. You are to run all the musical evenings at the White House. We'll open every one with "Die Wacht am Rhein", standing. After that a few blasts of Schubert, and then maybe some new songs. The beer must be kept not cooler than 40 degrees and not warmer than 50. I trust you to play fair in this matter, and not poison the Supreme Court. You'll have to get used to my accompaniments. Like Liszt, I sometimes strike a wrong note.

I went to N.Y. to dinner, got moderately tight, and remained over night at the Algonquin-Carleton. This morning I went to the office, struggled with mail for an hour, and then came home, snoozing all the way. It seemed short.

My best thanks for the Kellner article. Kellner, who is a professor doctor, is to translate "Notes on Democracy", though he will have to sign his daughter's name to it for academic reasons.[2] Also, there has been a row with the publisher, too complex to be set down.

I kiss your hand 17 times.

Yours,

M

G.H.: "*'You are to run all the musical evenings at the White House.'* See what I missed? I might have set the pace for 'real culture in the White House' long before Jacqueline Kennedy came along! What a loss!*"

1. The date here, which corresponds to that of the preceding letter, is clearly wrong. The envelope is postmarked November 1, 1927, and this letter recounts the trip to New York referred to as upcoming in the previous letter.

2. Leon Kellner taught at the University of Vienna and was the author of a short history of American literature that Mencken called "the best ever printed." The German translation of *Notes on Democracy*, attributed to Dora S. Kellner, was published in Berlin by Widerstands Verlag in 1930.

[T L S]   Baltimore
                                           November 2nd [1927]

Dear Gretchen:—

Is Longworth to be trusted? Don't forget that he is a candidate
himself.[1] It would be easy for him to slip a few drops of
aminoesterdibenzochloreolozin hypochlorite into my dram. He
looks honest, but it is certainly late in the day to be asking me to
trust politicians. But I trust your discretion.

I'll probably have to go to New York again next week. Our
annual meeting impends. I hope to have my salary raised to $15 a
week. The magazine is rolling in advertising, but getting it is
enormously expensive. The advertising department gives great
banquets, and I am not even invited. Such are the ways of business
in a republic of go-getters.

I am at work on my manifesto. It will be issued the day after
election day, 1928.

Your hand is kissed repeatedly.

                                           Yours,

                                           M

1. After Coolidge announced in August 1927 that he would not run again,
   Longworth was prominently mentioned as a presidential possibility.

[T L S]   Baltimore
                                           November 5th [1927]

Dear Gretchen:—

What you say of Longworth accords with the reports of my
operatives. I hear on all sides that he is a decent Christian man. Let
us try him out with nine highballs in nine minutes: the test of
theologians.

My announcement will certainly include you as Vice-President.
I'll probably never serve out even my first term. The cares of state
will reduce me to a cinder. Thus you will go down into history
along with Elizabeth, Victoria and the Queen of the Amazons.

You waste time on Bodenheim.[1] Let him wash his neck, and I'll
be glad to meet him. But I hate dirty geniuses.

Richard Trunk is a new one to me.[2] The beer has been bad in
Berlin since the war, and the music written there shows it.

I kiss your hand!

Yours,

M

1. Bodenheim, whose literary and financial fortunes were usually in a pre-
   carious state, evidently switched in his communications with Hood from
   being argumentative to importuning her to intercede for him with
   Mencken.
2. German composer and conductor, known for his choral music and lieder.

[TLS]   Baltimore
                                        November 12th [1927]

Dear Gretchen:—

Your letter followed me up to Babylon and then down again. A
round of dinners, with a trip into Westchester, where Knopf is
building a palace. He has a music room as big as the Union
Station, and will put in five pianos. Let us give a recital in it when
it is ready. It will take 3000 men until 1929 to complete the house,
swimming-pool, polo-grounds, private steeple-chase, etc.

I have not read the Sinclair piece.[1] Poor Upton! A charming
fellow, but very credulous. He always falls for quacks. Now one of
them has given him a fine ulcer on the sole of one of his feet, and
he is on crutches, and will remain on them for months. It never
occurs to him to go to a good doctor.

Tell Bodenheim that I'll be glad to lend him $10 at 5% a month,
if he can induce Louis Untermeyer, Spingarn and Liveright to
endorse his note.[2] His sufferings really touch me. Villon went
through nothing comparable to them: he always had plenty of vin
rouge. But think of starving sober!

I am in my usual mess. God, what a life! I am quitting the Tribune to get some air.[3]

And kiss your hand furiously.

Yours,

M

1. Probably Sinclair's "Mr. Mencken Calls on Me," in the November *Bookman*.
2. Literary critic Joel Spingarn and Bodenheim's publisher, Horace Liveright.
3. Mencken's syndicated *Chicago Tribune* articles were terminated in January 1928.

[TLS]   Baltimore
                                        November 14th [1927]

Dear Gretchen:—

Our letters crossed. The week [in] New York was a heavy one, with a great deal of gadding about and too much gin. I am here now trying to clear off my desk. On Friday I must go to the Eastern Shore for a stag party—an annual affair, with the Chief Justice of Maryland as the main guest.[1] From there I shall go up to West Chester to visit Hergesheimer for two days. Then home, and more labor. And then New York again. I feel like a squirrel in a cage.

But the end is in sight. Beginning January 1st I'll be in easier waters. I am giving up the Tribune stuff, and have arranged with the Evening Sun for less work. My plan is to devote the whole of 1928 to my book.[2] That will take me to Washington often, to work in the library. If you are really a Christian woman you will let me see you.

I hesitate to suggest a date for the Longworth party for the above reasons. But maybe I'll be able to come over next week. More anon.

How many geological epochs is it since I saw you last? It must have been in Paleolithic times.

Yours,

M

1. A gathering in Easton, Maryland, hosted by lawyer Daniel M. Henry, to feast on terrapin and seafood. The Chief Justice of Maryland was Carroll Taney Bond.
2. *Treatise on the Gods.*

[TLS]   [Baltimore]
November 26th [1927]

Dear Gretchen:—

December 7th will be excellent for your humble slave, either for lunch or for dinner. And either in Baltimore or in Washington. Let me know what Longworth says, and I'll be ready. I suggest that dinner may be better than lunch. Let me hear from you at 730 Fifth avenue. I'll be there until Thursday.

Woollcott seems to be making good progress.[1] He is now devouring and retaining ice-cream, and is lifted to an angle of 20 degrees to get it down. In a couple of weeks he should be sitting up. The Twelve Apostles made a furious grab for him. I incline to think, indeed, that SS. Luke and Mark actually had him by the tail. But he shook them off, and got away.

My chaplain has had five more kicks in the pantaloons to remind him that Hazel must, will and shall win.[2] Have no fear! When he spits on his hands he is irresistable. I have promised him a case of cut Scotch if he does a good job. Sound liquor would be wasted on him.

I have been approached by gentlemen who want me to run for the Senate next year. I have told them that I have Larger Plans.

La Gilfond's amours are hard to follow. Why should she leave that perfectly good husband? Certainly it must be more comfortable to have a sound husband in the house than to go sky-hooting over the world with a lover. Is she a movie-fan? I hope not. The other day I bought another article from her.[3]

And now, herewith, kiss your hand.

Yours,

M

The letter is written on stationery which Mencken had made up with an elaborate letterhead for a fictitious organization, the American Institute of Arts and Letters (Colored). Another of the jokes he indulged in with his correspondents, it exemplifies, as do his cards for the Kosher Chinese restaurant and the multitalented Rev. Mandolowitz, how much the racial and ethnic staples of American humor infused his sense of the comical.

1. Mencken had written Hood on November 18 that the author of "I Am a 100% American" had been hospitalized with a severe stomach ailment.

2. Hazel Arth, Hood's student, sang in the first national radio competition for vocalists sponsored by the Atwater Kent Foundation, with Hood accompanying her on the piano. Arth did not win this time, but won in 1928.

3. Duff Gilfond's "The White Ribboners," a satiric examination of the WCTU, appeared in the March 1928 *American Mercury*.

[TLS]   Baltimore
                                         December 3rd [1927]

Dear Gretchen:—

Very good. I'll wait on you at 4 precisely on Wednesday. Let us embalm Mr. Speaker for the orgies at the Palace, and then go to dinner at the Grand Café Madrillon. I'll bring along a butt of malmsey. You will be shocked to see me. I have aged dreadfully, and my new china teeth are very uncomfortable.

I refused the Gridiron Club invitation (which was not formal) simply because I had always refused in the past, and never go to public dinners if I can help it. It was sent to me because the club wanted to show that there were no hard feelings over the Raymond Tompkins article. But I care nothing for hard feelings. I have known many of the Gridiron brethren for years, and am fond of them, but I hate public orgies.[1]

I kiss your hand.

Yours in Xt.,

M

1. The dinners of the Gridiron Club are major Washington social events, at which members (a select group of Washington correspondents) perform songs and skits spoofing national political figures and affairs. In October, the *Mercury* had carried Raymond S. Tompkins' "Princes of the Press," a good-humored deflation of the legend of the Gridiron Club and the journalistic mystique surrounding the Washington press corps.

[ALS]   New York
          [December 1, 1927]

Dear Gretchen:

I am all set for the 7th—lunch or dinner. If the Polizei forbid the party will you let me have word at Baltimore? Why not meet at the Madrillon? We can get a private-room. Or have you another scheme?

You are completely incomparable. History will put you beside Nancy Hanks[1] and Martha Washington. As for me, I fear my class will be that of Fall, Doheny,[2] and Sacco and Vanzetti.

Yours,

M

1. Mother of Abraham Lincoln.
2. Albert B. Fall, Harding's Secretary of the Interior, and oilman Edward L. Doheny were the principal culprits in the Tea Pot Dome scandal.

[TLS]   Baltimore
                                                     Thursday
                                                     [December 8, 1927]

Dear Gretchen:—

The party was lovely, and so were you. I rolled in at 1.15 feeling
very mellow, and have a vague fogginess in my head this morning.
God will reward you! When are you going to let me come again?

By this mail I am sending you a little ivory box. I hope it fits
your other trappings. The lady whose portrait appears on the top I
knew well. She suffered misfortunates late in life, and they ravaged
her beauty.

The box is NOT a Christmas present. I abhor Christmas, and
prohibit Christmas presents under dreadful penalties.

Ich kuss die Hand.

                                                     Yours,

                                                     M

G.H.: " 'The party' began here with cocktails: Mencken, Nick Longworth, his secty, Lucille [McArthur] (widow of rep. Pat [Clifton Nesmith]
McArthur of Oregon) and myself. We first stopped at Poli's Theater, where
John Charles Thomas was rehearsing with Wash. Opera Co. for 'Thaïs' &
tried to drag him out to dinner with us.[1] John had been a good pal of mine
since I met him, around 1918. But he was all togged out (dress rehearsal)
in monk's costume & almost wept because he couldn't make it. His eyes
fairly popped when I walked in with 2 other celebrities Longworth and
Mencken. Later, we dined at Madrillon. Fun, songs & witty sayings flew
thick & fast. What an evening for a most proper gal!"

1. Thomas was a highly popular American baritone.

[TLS]   Baltimore
                                                     Thursday
                                                     [December 15, 1927]

Dear Gretchen:—

Very good! I'll be here on the 26th, 27th, 28th, 29th and 30th. Let
me hear the date as soon as Mr. Speaker decides. I suggest that we

meet at the Rennert Palace Hotel at 6.30 or thereabout, take on a few modest stimulants, and then sit down to the victuals.[1] The hotel will do a good job, but it ought to have several days' notice.

I shall begin drawing up my platform anon. On this I must have your advise and help. What shall I say about Farm Relief? Shall we let the farmers starve peacefully, or send out the Army to butcher them? I can't make up my mind.[2]

I went to a dinner of doctors last night, and had *one* cocktail— no more! It was dreadful. I am still in a low and pessimistic state.

Yours,

M

1. Mencken had written two days earlier to propose a dinner with Long-worth at the Rennert, long one of his favorite dining places in Baltimore.
2. On December 17 Mencken sent Hood an article from the December 21 issue of the *New Republic* with this comment: "To Hell with Hearst. Look at the enclosed. Your prayers are beginning to fetch the heavenly host." The article attacked the prevailing hypocrisy among politicians of both parties toward Prohibition. To make the 1928 campaign an honest politi-cal forum on the issue, the editors fancifully proposed two presidential tickets: for the Republicans, Senator William E. Borah and Gifford Pin-chot, both staunch supporters of vigorous enforcement of the Volstead Act; for the Democrats, Nicholas Murray Butler, President of Columbia University and a conservative Republican but a proponent of repeal of the Eighteenth Amendment, and Henry L. Mencken ("Prohibition as an Issue," pp. 128–30; copy in Mencken/Hood Collection).

[TLS]   Baltimore
Friday [December 23, 1927]

Dear Gretchen:—

Let me hear about the Longworth party as soon as you can. I am keeping Wednesday and Thursday evenings clear. Tell Longworth that under no circumstances is he to dress. The waiters at the one-armed lunch where we are to victual would shoot a man in dress clothes. The place is rough, but they give large portions.

I have had a horrible week in New York, with too many dinners and too little sleep. I got home last night to find my desk piled mountain high. It will be Christmas night before I get to the bottom of the pile. Thus God punishes those who neglect the sacraments.

Both your hands are kissed.

Yours,

M

On this same day, Mencken sent Hood the following telegram: "The heroic boys of the fleet have just made a safe landing and I am hard at work getting my share. It includes some superb museum pieces. Let us have a look at them next week. A happy Christmas."

G.H.: *"This refers to booze brought in for his Longworth party."*

[TLS]   Baltimore
                                         December 26th [1927]

Dear Gretchen:—

It is too damned bad, but such are God's ways. His will, not ours, be done. On January 8th I'll have to be in New York and on the 11th I'll probably leave for Havana.[1] It has been impossible to get accomodations on the 14th or 12th, and I refuse to move on the 13th, which is a Friday. But I'll be here on the 2nd, 3rd, 4th, 5th and 6th, and if Longworth can come on any of those days let me know and I'll have the wild terrapin put on the fire.

The Graphic report puzzles me.[2] I can't identify the lady. Can it be Ruth Suckow?[3] She is a Christian woman, and the daughter of a high-toned clergyman. I fear her pa will forbid the banns.

I spent a very sober Christmas. From dawn to dark I got down exactly one cocktail, a half bottle of Piesporter Olk 1921, and five Scotch highballs. I become abstemious in my old age. Well, I must conserve my health for the national service. Don't forget that Harding went on the water-wagon in his last days. My father used to drink a whole bowl of egg-nogg on Christmas, not to mention five or six whiskeys, a bottle of bad Rhine wine, and half a case of beer.

If I visit your great city next week will you have lunch with me? Borras reports that his new Madrillon is very swell.

Yours,

M

1. Mencken was to cover the sixth Pan American Conference for the *Evening Sun.*

2. The *New York Daily Graphic,* Bernarr MacFadden's tabloid, evidently carried an article (not located) mentioning rumors of marriage about Mencken.

3. Midwestern fiction writer, whose career Mencken launched in the *Smart Set.*

[TLS]   Baltimore
                              December 28th [1927]

Dear Gretchen:—

It is a canard, set going by the Hoover outfit. The gal you mention was married four or five years ago, and at last accounts was living in Paris.[1] She had high designs for me: she wanted me to go into the movies.

Will Monday be convenient for lunch? I am on the trail of a Cuban woman lawyer, and must see her before I go to Havana. I'll take her on late in the afternoon.

Beware of Sazarac cocktails. They are full of absinthe and cause female weakness in its worst forms.

I have a sore throat, a pain in the back, and a game leg. Such are the fruits of sobriety. It is not natural to my constitution.

I am holding January 6th open. It is Friday.

Yours,

M

1. Hood had in all likelihood named Marion Bloom as a possible candidate for "the lady" in the "Graphic report," whom Mencken could not identify in his previous letter. His close relationship with Bloom had ended when she abruptly married in 1923 and went to live in France.

[T L S]   Baltimore
                                     December 30th [1927]

Dear Gretchen:—

It now turns out that it will be a physical impossibility for me to
get to Washington on Monday. I am simply flooded by visitors, and
some of them I can't dodge. But I am clearing Friday the 6th, and
shall make no engagement for it whatsoever. I suggest meeting at
the Rennert at 6.30 or thereabout. I'll get a room, and bring along
such wines as you have not seen for years. There is an ante-chamber
attached, and in it a small retiring room for our distinguished
guest. The victuals at the Rennert are superb, perhaps the best in
America. Don't eat any lunch. You will take aboard at least 20,000
calories.

Shall we have a radio in the White House? It would be polite,
but I am against it.

From one who kisses your hand.

                                     Yours,

                                     M

[T L S]   Baltimore
                                     January 2nd [1928]

Dear Gretchen:—

All is set for a refined affair on Thursday. I'll look for you at the
Rennert Hotel at 7 P.M. Come in the ladies' entrance on Saratoga
street, and I'll be in attendance. NO DRESSING. I shall wear the
ordinary habiliments of a Christian patriot. If there is any
impediment wire me at once, so that I can call off the cooks and
vintners. I promise you a very high-toned programme of wines and
liquors, all out of my private cellars.

Carl Van Vechten and his wife, Fania Marinoff, are here.[1] I put
in the evening with them yesterday. Getting home, I was dam nigh
frozen. The temperature here is 35 degrees below zero, and a 100-
mile gale is blowing. Ships have been blown up out of the harbor
into the middle of the town. All around me I hear the yells of

people freezing to death. The local Ku Klux has forbidden the A.P. to send out this news.

I kiss your hand.

Yours,

M

1. Van Vechten was a popular novelist of the twenties; his wife was an actress.

[T L S]   Baltimore
                                             Wednesday [January 4, 1928]

Dear Gretchen:—

The stalled ox is on the fire, and the wood alcohol is bubbling in the still. I shall look for you at 7 P.M. Come to the Saratoga street entrance. We'll be waited on by Boston, the king of waiters. He won the Police Gazette diamond belt in 1889.[1]

I enclose your cards of admission.[2]

Yours,

M

1. A prize-fighting trophy.
2. Mencken enclosed three bottle labels from imported beers and ales, inscribed in ink: "Admit one Jan. 5 '28 HLM" (in Mencken/Hood Collection).

[T L S (postscript handwritten)]   Baltimore
                                          January 7th [1928]

Dear Gretchen:—

I am engaging Boston, the king of waiters, by the year. Name the date, and the next party will be called. I suspect that I was in my cups toward the end, but surely I had a glorious time. You were colossal. I stayed in that saloon only 20 minutes. Then to bed.

I have a pain in the throat, and am to see a quack this afternoon. It has been annoying me for 10 days. It seems to be deep down,

half way to the gizzard. But I must go to New York tomorrow.
Such is the fortitude of a war hero.
    Ich kuss die Hand!

                            Yours,

                            HLM

I don't believe a word of it. Jack Gilbert tells me that you say
precisely the same thing to him.[1]

    G.H.: *"Yes, he was 'in his cups toward the end.' He gave us each a very
specially bound red leather & gilt copy of Selected Prejudices—& inscribed
mine in such a drunken hand I defy anybody to read what he wrote."
(Hood apparently misremembers. In an earlier letter, not included here,
Mencken mentions having sent her* Selected Prejudices. *On a Xerox
copy of the present letter, she writes, "He gave me a de-luxe copy of
[Schimpflexicon] & the scrawling of my name was illegible. 'In hopes'
however, was clear." Mencken probably gave them advance copies of* Menckeniana: A Schimpflexicon, *which was published two weeks later.) "We
got home safely, but not without Nick making a few passes at me—and
with Lucille [McArthur] on his other side!! He was surely 'lit up' to a
fare-thee-well. Lucille kept sober by running into the lavatory every so
often, sticking her finger down her throat, upchucking everything & coming out, smiling & starting to drink all over again! Never heard of such a
life-saver, but it worked with her."*

1. John Gilbert was Valentino's successor as the great lover of the silent
   screen. In "The Low-Down on Hollywood," Mencken facetiously confessed to being jealous of the film star's attraction for women (*Photoplay*
   [April 1927], p. 37).

[ALS]   New York
                                 [January 11, 1928]

Dear Gretchen:
    This literary life will kill me yet. Last night I dined with the
Boyds, and acquired a most magnificent slant.[1] Such debaucheries
must cease. If I am to save the Republic in 1932 I must swallow less
poison. Poor Judd Gray!

My throat seems to be better. The treatment made it far worse for 3 or 4 days, but now it is fairly comfortable. Let me have your prayers.

Ruth, alas, must die! I have done my damndest for her, but to no avail. I hear she will pass away in the full hope of a glorious resurrection. Be warned![2]

From one who kisses your hand.

M

G.H.: *"Of one thing I'm certain: if he had quit overloading his poor tummy with booze & rich foods, long ago, he'd be alive today. He went, far too young & could have managed on a few drinks a day—not all that stuff he crammed down his gullet!"*

1. Ernest Boyd, critic and free-lance writer, and his wife, Madeleine, long-time friends of Mencken. In 1925 Boyd wrote one of the first books on Mencken.

2. Henry Judd Gray and Ruth Brown Snyder were executed at Sing-Sing on January 12, 1928, for the murder of her husband, Albert Snyder, on March 20, 1927. The details of their crime, their trial and conviction, and their punishment—including Mrs. Snyder's conversion to Catholicism while in prison—gained nationwide notoriety in the press.

   Mencken's reference to Gray in connection with his own overindulgence at dinner perhaps stems from his earlier ruminations on the case. His Monday article for March 28, 1927, entitled "Poor Technique," took the crude bludgeoning of Albert Snyder as the jumping-off point for a satiric disquisition on the prevalence of undetected domestic murders. A wife's already ample opportunities to dispatch her husband subtly with poison had become greater and safer, Mencken averred, now that Prohibition made tainted alcohol commonplace and wives adept at "the new science of domestic bartending."

[TLS]   Baltimore
                                               January 14th [1928]

Dear Gretchen:—

You are to call me Mr. Mencken! Or Herr Mencken. I have long carried on a campaign against women calling men of years and learning by their first names. Even wives should not be permitted to do it. Mrs. Washington called Washington General. But despite the rule I waive it in your case. You are a licensed outlaw.

My sympathy went, not to La Snyder, but to poor Judd Gray. He was a good man, and he was brought to his death by the best of intentions. His last words greatly affected me. I shall have them reprinted in a small pamphlet, as a warning to young men.[1]

I hate compromises, and so can't follow Lindsey. His companionate idea is simply tosh. Marriage is a magnificent banality, but the only way to make it bearable is to admit the fact. Every evasion makes it ridiculous.[2]

I am off to the Havana this evening. My address there will be the Plaza Hotel. I hear that it is a swell place. But the work promises to be unpleasant.

Houston in June![3] I'll have a roaring time there. All the evangelists in the South will be on the job.

Ich kuss die Hand!

Yours,

M

G.H.: *"I began to call him Harry."*

1. Gray's last words reputedly were "I hope that my example will be a warning to others and that some who are going wrong will change their rudder and keep off the rocks."

   Mencken's expressed view of Gray gave an ironic twist to the conventional formula of "the good man gone wrong": he pictured Gray as a naively virtuous man whose lapse into adultery so convinced him of his essential sinfulness that he was unable to see any difference between that transgression and the act of murder to which he was thus easily led by Mrs. Snyder. ("A Good Man Gone Wrong" [review of Gray's *Doomed Ship*], *American Mercury* [Feb. 1929], pp. 254–55.)

2. Judge Ben B. Lindsey's recently published *The Companionate Marriage*, coauthored by Wainwright Evans, had aroused an immediate public outcry. Lindsey advocated, as an alternative to procreative marriage, the companionate ideal, buttressed by legalized birth control and the right of childless couples to divorce by mutual consent, normally with no alimony. He insisted that companionate marriage was neither "free love" nor "trial marriage," but many attackers lumped all these ideas together as nothing more than promiscuity. Mencken had just published two pieces on Lindsey's ideas. Reviewing the book for the January *Mercury*, he dis-

missed the fulminations against Lindsey as so much cant, but expressed his own reservations as to the Judge's optimism about ameliorating marital unhappiness. In his January 8 *Chicago Tribune* article, he contended that the concept of companionate marriage undermined, rather than improved, mutual trust and served a sound union worse than traditional monogamy.

3. Mencken's Monday article for January 16 applauded Houston as the site of the upcoming Democratic National Convention: "I confess frankly that the choice of the Texas city . . . pleases me immensely. . . . It will be an instructive experience to fry and boil through two weeks of a Texas June, with a red-hot sun overhead and the boll-weevils buzzing in the air. And it will be educational, too, to see the Texas Democrats—a hearty and hospitable race of men, with hair on their chests, three-gallon hats, and such confidence in Holy Writ as one finds in the North only in gentlemen awaiting execution."

[TLS]

Plaza Hotel
Havana, Cuba
Friday [January 20, 1928]

Dear Gretchen:—

The show has blown up, and I am coming home.[1] I should be in Baltimore by Tuesday. It has been hard work in the hot sun, and so I have got down very little liquor. But tonight I hope to drink at least 30 Seidel of beer.

I am amazed by what you say of our eminent friend.[2] It shocks me first to hear that he forgets himself, and secondly that a poor working girl should be blind to the great honor he does her. How many women have been necked by *two* candidates for the sacred office?

Coolidge made a great hit here. They expected him to be even worse.

Tomorrow the Havana literati are giving me a lunch party. I shall wear all my orders.

A sweaty, unpleasant place. I long for Schellhase's saloon in Baltimore.[3] There is nothing like it here. The local beer is third-rate, and the imported German stuff is bilge.

I kiss your hand.

Yours,

M

1. On January 17 Mencken had written Hood from Havana: "The show here is the usual horrible imbecility. Trust the boys in spats to make it so!" The United States made the Pan American Conference a major diplomatic event. President Coolidge visited Havana to address the opening session on January 16, and the U.S. delegation, headed by Charles Evans Hughes, was generally considered the most prestigious one sent to an international conference up to that time, except for the one which attended the negotiations of the Treaty of Versailles. Mencken's articles for the *Evening Sun* viewed the Pan American meetings as a polite and formal extravaganza which left the real issues of U.S.–Latin American relations untouched.

2. Nicholas Longworth.

3. Mencken prized Schellhase's, then located on Franklin Street, for its food and its atmosphere, but foremost for its excellent beer.

[T L S (postscript handwritten in upper left corner)]

Baltimore
January 27th [1928]

Dear Gretchen:—

By God's infinite mercy I have got home safely. It was a dreadful experience. The beer turned out to be bilge—even the so-called German beer, which came from Hamburg and Bremen, two sink-holes. I was bilious in six hours, but had to stick to it. I found very little good wine. The tourists demand champagne, and the Cubans seem to be content with grocery-store Ponet Canet, and such garbage. The best I found was my old friend, Castell del Remy—Spanish and cheap, but very sound. I found only two really good restaurants. As for the Conference, it turned out a flop. The moment the Nicaraguans, Haitians, etc., caught sight of Hughes' whiskers their livers turned to water.[1] Enough of such sad things.

My desk is a sight. I dictated at least 100 letters this morning, and the whole place is still awash. I have enough MSS. to read to last me until the Second Coming.

I still think you are unappreciative of Nick. You gals are all too sniffish. He is one of the greatest Americans of his time, and yet you gag when he tries to neck you. Suppose Aimee McPherson were to tackle me?[2] Do you think I'd complain? By no means. It might make me suffer spiritually, but I'd think of the honor.

Very soon I hope to visit your great city. When I get this sand out of my eyes. Meanwhile, I kiss your hand, whether you yell or not.

Yours,

M

Broun is right. He was aiming at Bodenheim.[3]

1. Hughes sought to mollify Latin-American resentment against the recent intervention of U.S. marines in Nicaragua and their presence in Haiti.
2. Mencken's visit to the temple of Aimee Semple McPherson in Los Angeles, a highspot of his trip to California in 1926, convinced him that her sex appeal was the secret of her success as an evangelist.
3. The comment is obscure. None of Broun's recent columns in the *New York World* or the *Nation* make direct or clearly implied reference to Bodenheim.

[TLS]   New York [Baltimore]
                                                       January 31st [1928]

Dear Gretchen:—

Beware of drunken women! The last one I tackled bit me in the ear, and it took 13 stictches to restore me. I'd almost rather fight a Siberian wolf. The language they use is dreadful. Nothing worse comes from Sunday-school superintendents under ether.

I am dam nigh frozen. One of The Sun men got home from Havana in the very midst of the blizzard. A single blast of it sent him to bed, and he is there yet. I got in the day before it cut loose, and have not succumbed, but I am still shivering.

I observe that Young Teddy Rosenfeldt is on the stump against Al Smith.[1] What a lucky fellow Al is! We must try to inveighle Teddy into doing it all over again in 1932. It would be a pleasure and an honor to run against him.

More when I freeze out. The temperaure is less than 20.

Yours,

M

1. Having lost the New York gubernatorial election in 1924 to Smith, the son of President Theodore Roosevelt (and brother-in-law of Nicholas Longworth) was making speeches attacking Smith as a presidential candidate with an eye toward running again for governor or gaining the Republican nomination for Vice-President.

[ALS]

Hotel Algonquin
New York
[February 6, 1928]

Dear Gretchen:

Beware of Fred Essary.[1] He is a dangerous man. I could tell you tales that [would] make you shrink. Compared to him His Excellency[2] is an amateur.

I shall come to the Mayflower Hotel recital, and hide behind a palm. If you do well you will hear some beery hochs from there. But if you gurgle and gargle I'll upset the palm and so bust up the show. Don't forget that I am an old music critic, and perhaps the best heard of since Schumann. My specialty in the old days was reviewing concerts of Sousa's band. I had to quit when I grew somewhat deaf.

New York is really wonderful. I have been seeing the sights all day—the aquarium, the Woollworth Tower, Grant's Tomb, etc. Fifth avenue is a very swell street. But the Algonquin Palace hotel seems gloomy without you.

I kiss your hand.

Yours in Xt

HLM

1. J. Frederick Essary was chief of the Washington bureau for the *Baltimore Sun*.
2. One of Mencken's sobriquets for Longworth; others are "His Eminence" and "The Professor."

[T L S]   Baltimore
                                           February 9th [1928]

Dear Gretchen:—

Let us take on La Guardia, by all means. Will he come to
Baltimore? If so, I'll arrange a session at the Rennert Palace Hotel.
Tell him he must haul you here and back, and give bond that he
will attempt no necking. The fourth member of the party I leave to
you. La Gilfond rather alarms me, but I leave it to you. I'll be here
for two weeks.

You vastly underestimate yourself. You are worth all of the
Algonquin gals, whether in the films or not. I never look at them.
There was a time when I did, but that was long ago.

I have just got in from New York, and find the usual mountain
of mail. Included in it are dozens of letters that went to Havana
and missed me. I suspect the Cuban spies of holding them up and
reading them.

I suppose you know that Essary is an earnest Christian man. In
fact, I have seen the pond in Tennessee where he was baptized.

                                           Yours,

                                           M

[T L S]   Baltimore
                                           February 10th [1928]

Dear Gretchen:—

Your poetical gifts knock me cold. Not since Charles K. Harris
has America seen one with talents for both words and music.[1] I am
proud to have such a lady friend.

The quacks are still monkeying with my throat. It is not painful,
but very uncomfortable. They agree only on one thing: that
nothing is to be done about it. Meanwhile, I curse them in the
privacy of my chamber.

I kiss your hand!

                                           Yours,

                                           M

Two red paper hearts, cut in a lacy pattern, are glued to the top of this letter and overlay the text, while three Valentine stickers appear beneath it and another decorates the envelope.

In response to a Valentine, signed "Otto," which Mencken had sent her, Hood wrote him the following poem:

> I'm "lucky to have such a beau"
> My boy friend reminded me of it;
> But when he would prove that it's so,
> He grows shy, and God, how I love it!
> He's shy and he's sweet and he's low,
> To please me he should use a club.
> Be my cave-man, my passionate pink glow
> That follows my cold morning tub!

(Mencken's card and a copy of Hood's poem are in the Mencken/Hood Collection.)

---

1. Popular songwriter at the turn of the century. In another letter, dated February 14, Mencken added: "Charles K. Harris is one of my favorite poets. Have you ever given a prayerful reading to 'After the Ball'? It is really swell stuff."

[TLS]   Baltimore
                                               Wednesday
                                               [February 15, 1928]

Dear Gretchen:—

La Guardia sounds like a Christian of Apostolic times. Does he chew tobacco? If not, I shall teach him. A Sunday night would be excellent. I suggest Sunday, March 4th: a fateful day. Let us think of five years hence. If not a wop in the White House, then why not one in the Cabinet?[1]

I spent six hours yesterday making out my income tax return. John D. Rockefeller himself could not have made heavier weather of it. It now turns out that I must pay taxes on a good year during a lean year. By October I'll be in the almshouse.

I am off to see my lawyer.

Yours,

M

1. La Guardia, an excellent cook, had undertaken to host their party in Washington and to prepare a sumptuous dinner.

[TLS]   Baltimore
                                   Saturday [February 18, 1928]

Dear Gretchen:—

I surely hope your mother is much better. If you are as jumpy as I am when there is illness in the house, then you are having a horrible time. Tell her that if she doesn't obey orders I shall complain to the police. If necessary, strap her in bed.

I trust you to make delicate inquiries into the La Guardia business. We must think, not of ourselves, but of our country. Drinking high-balls at dinner would light up my old Bright's disease, and maybe bump me off. Let it be hinted that I am a fan for sound Italian wines. The redder the better.

You are to drink that Erdener Treppchen at once! It was for your own lily-white gills, not for guests. As for the St. Julian, it is probably corked long ago. It never keeps.

I shall wait on the invalid tomorrow morning, and find out what the quacks did to her.[1] I'll be back at work Monday morning at 7.30.

The Broun thing is in very bad taste.[2]

Yours,

M

1. Blanche Knopf, Alfred Knopf's wife and business partner, was hospitalized in New York.

2. Mencken probably refers to Heywood Broun's disparaging comments on George Jean Nathan in his "It Seems to Me" column in the *New York World* on February 16. Broun held a particularly jaundiced view of writing about the theater, and he took Nathan and his most recent collection of essays, *Art of the Night,* as a case in point. Broun penned what amounted to almost a literary obituary of Nathan by explicitly contrasting him to Mencken:

> Some fifteen years ago, or maybe it was twenty, George Jean Nathan wrote a mannered prose all jetted with a wit which flashed in any lamplight. The public spoke then of "Mencken and Nathan." That phrase has gone. Mencken has stolen too many laps on his competitor and comrade. I am inclined to think that Nathan's gift was always slighter, but the present margin of difference would not be anything like so great had the contest been a fair one. Mencken took for his field books, music, politics, medicine and life in general. Nathan stuck to the theater and got bogged there.

Although Mencken and Nathan had become personally distant since 1925, when Nathan's role at the *Mercury* was curtailed to contributing editor, Mencken may have found distasteful the holding up of his own example to demean his erstwhile friend and co-editor.

[TLS]   Baltimore
                                                      March 2, 1928.

Dear Gretchen:

I have a long letter from one Levi Cooke, a friend of Mrs. McArthur, protesting that if I print an article about Mrs. Willebrandt it ought to be more or less favorable. I am telling him that the matter is out of my hands and that La Gilfond is authorized to write whatever she pleases. It wouldn't do, of course, for The American Mercury to print an eulogy of the lady but I certainly see no reason why we shouldn't say she has merit when she really has.[1]

The quacks tell me that they'll finish with me in 24 hours. Thus I should be on my merry way by Tuesday morning. The operation will be absurdly trivial. Unfortunately, it will require me to spend a night in the hospital listening to the groans of the other customers. I shall take along a Bible and devote the evening to serious reading.

I incline to think that Sunday a week will be too early for the La

Guardia party. But unluckily I can't tell you positively at the moment. I'll write you again early next week.

Yours,

M

1. Mabel Walker Willebrandt was Assistant Attorney-General of the United States (1921–29) and chief architect of the government's enforcement of the Prohibition laws and prosecution of violators. In 1928, as a strong Hoover partisan and head of the Committee on Credentials, she was the foremost woman participant at the Republican Convention.

An article on Willebrandt, "Portia in Wonderland," appeared in the *Mercury* in July 1929, with its author designated only as "a Washington correspondent." Tracing the series of cases which Willebrandt had argued before the Supreme Court, the article claimed that "more than any other jurisconsult in America, she has put the kibosh on the Bill of Rights."

Levi Cooke, a prominent Washington attorney, was for many years the general counsel for the National Wholesale Liquor Dealers' Association.

[TLS]   Baltimore
                                       Tuesday [March 6, 1928]

Dear Gretchen:—

God has delivered me from the clutches of those grave-robbers. Yesterday morning they gouged out [my] left tonsil hole, and this morning they cut two small moles off my breast. All the tissues removed turned out to be absolutely benign, and so I am feeling very good. My tongue is still swollen a bit, but I can eat. I should be back to complete normalcy in a week.

More anon. You are dear to be so concerned. Tell His Eminence that without prayer I would have despaired.

Yours,

M

Hood had sent the following telegram to Mencken in the hospital: "If you don't recover I'll follow you; if you do I'll leave you alone. Gretchen" (copy of text in Mencken/Hood Collection).

[TLS]   Baltimore
                                             March 11th [1928]

Dear Gretchen:—
   It is lucky I am not trying to get down La Guardia's chow
tonight. My throat is still very sore. But the lassitude that went
with it is passing off, and I begin to feel almost normal again. The
next time I'll be more careful.
   The quacks tell me that my voice will be greatly improved. For
eight or ten years past I have not been able to do justice to my low
notes. But now I'll be able to sing "Asleep in the Deep" again, and
maybe even "Im tiefen Keller"—my two favorites among all the
songs of Hugo Wolf.[1]
   My stenographer here, the best in America, breaks the news that
she is about to be married.[2] Worse, she is moving away. I'll be
hamstrung! God alone can save me.

                                             Yours,

                                             M

1. Late nineteenth-century Austrian composer, noted for his art songs.
   Mencken facetiously attributes to Wolf two popular bass solos.
2. Margaret Redding, his secretary in Baltimore since 1921.

[ALS]   New York
                                             [March 2-, 1928][1]

Dear Gretchen:
   This Harris-Ewing letter is superb.[2] Tell them to charge Spohn
$100 for the photograph, and offer to autograph it for $50
additional. The negative will be valuable after 1932.
   I slept 9 hours last night, and feel very lively today. I should be
back to normalcy in a week more. Put me down for the La Guardia
dinner Sunday a week.[3] All I ask is 1/2 a dozen bottles of wine.
   Somehow your story of that taxi bump seems incredible. I
marvel that you didn't break your neck. Get a good Jew lawyer and
sue everybody concerned. I surely hope you have recovered
completely. You are a bit vague about it.

I had dinner with two coons last night. They treated me very politely. Their prejudice against us white folks seems to be dying out.

From one who kisses your hand.

Yours,

M

1. This letter was evidently sent between March 20 and March 23. The second digit of the date is blurred on the postmark, but Mencken's previous letter (not included here) mentions his departure for New York on March 17, while the following letter is postmarked from Baltimore, March 23.
2. Hood had forwarded to Mencken a letter she had received from the Harris-Ewing Photographic News Service concerning a request for a picture of her from a collector of Menckeniana (letter in Mencken/Hood Collection).
3. The La Guardia dinner was now set for April 1.

[TLS]   Baltimore
                                     Friday [March 23, 1928]

Dear Gretchen:—

A world of woes and tribulations! That taxi business still makes me gasp. Have you seen a good quack? Such blows are not to be sniffed at. I hope there is no lingering headache.

The coons menace this neighborhood too. I don't care a damn myself, but while my mother lived it was serious. So I hired a Jew lawyer to induce the neighboring owners to sign an anti-coon agreement. The courts here have decided that it is legal. A few refused to sign, but I think I have enough to raise a horrible row if the crows actually try to move in. Maybe you could do the same thing in Washington. Have you consulted the neighbors in the block? There may be a lawyer among them.

I have been frightfully on the jump for ten days, on newspaper business. But now it promises to end.

Sunday a week we meet!

Yours,

M

G.H.: *"Should this be published now that the tide has turned?"*

Despite his statement that personally he didn't "care a damn" about having black neighbors, the overall tenor and tone of Mencken's remarks are hardly sympathetic to the idea. Clearly, his mind was divided. Not long after writing this letter, in two Monday articles deploring the decline of Baltimore's beauty and grace brought on by population growth and commercialism, he looked at the problem of changing neighborhoods as one of the many evidences. Here he addressed the two sides of the conflict more objectively. He did not fault the newcomers for the deterioration of an area that usually accompanied the shift in inhabitants. They had acquired older houses, and their straitened economic lot—not slovenly habits—prevented them from keeping up their homes. Those who had the wherewithal maintained their property as well as their white counterparts. No one, he claimed, begrudged black Baltimoreans "their deliverance from unutterable slums." However, Mencken also argued that the white homeowner could not be expected to forget what the black advance cost him. "His house, menaced, declines rapidly in value. His neighbors, in a panic, sell out to the harpies who prey upon both whites and blacks." Not surprisingly, the real culprits in this dilemma were, for Mencken, the agents of "progress" and the "go-getter" mentality that infested contemporary American life. ("Smoke" and "Changing Baltimore," *Baltimore Evening Sun,* 7 May 1928 and 17 Dec. 1928.)

[TLS]   Baltimore
                                                  April 2, 1928.

Dear Gretchen:

I am sorry indeed that I was in such a low state last night. I shouldn't have gone to Washington at all, but after failing at the last moment three times running I was determined to do so. I feel much better today, though I am still very shaky. More anon.

                                    Yours,

                                    M

G.H.: *"La Guardia set a wopping feast—but M. was not well and couldn't really get going. Felt so sorry for him. La Gilfond drove him to train but I remained there with our host La G. which was the only proper thing to do, since M. left early & suddenly."*

[A L S]   New York [Baltimore]
                                               [April 21, 1928]

Dear Gretchen:

I protest violently against all such follies. You forget completely your duty to the Republic. Moreover I refuse absolutely to believe that you went to San Diego. You really flew to College Park, Md. I got no souvenir post-cards. Where are your proofs? Remember Dr. Cook and his fate![1]

My sister-in-law is back in Pittsburgh, and for the moment, at least, no quacks haunt the house. But I am not optimistic.

I am going to Boston tomorrow night. I have 17 engagements there Monday. Let me have your prayers.

From one who kisses your hand

HLM

1. Arctic explorer Frederick Cook's claim to have discovered the North Pole was not recognized because of insufficient confirming evidence.

[T L S]   Baltimore
                                               April 26th [1928]

Dear Gretchen:—

I'll believe it when I get an affidavit from Colonel Reynolds, witnessed by Lindbergh Himself.[1] If I hadda heard of it in time Ida set the cops on you, and had you lodged in the District gow. The ideer! Do you want me to be scared to death in the White House? No postcard from San Diego has come in.

I had a roaring time in Boston, and got back to New York

somewhat weary. Now I face a week of continuous visitors. What a life!

More anon. I am just in from New York.

Yours,

M

1. *G.H.:* "Can't recall at this remote date, who 'Reynolds' was!" He was evidently involved with her flying trip.

[T L S]

Baltimore
April 29th [1928]

Dear Gretchen:—

Now I begin to have doubts about even Reynolds. I hear that he is a violator of the Volstead Act. Tell him to get at least four witnesses, including one clergyman.

I have been in my usual whirl. Jim Tully is here, and came to my house last night.[1] It was the regular Saturday night beer party. He made a great hit with the brethren, who had never seen such a fellow before. Today I have him for lunch. On Wednesday Dr. Logan Clendening, author of "The Human Body" is coming for dinner.[2] He will know a great deal more about the human body after he sees the other guests fall upon the wines and liquors. Others are in the offing.

There is a movement to throw the Tom Walsh delegates to me at Houston. But I refuse to have anything to do with McAdoo men. McAdoo is one of my pet aversions. If he were Pope I'd refuse to let him shrive me.[3]

Knopf is in Washington today listening to the concerts at the Library of Congress. But Tully's presence makes it impossible for me to come over. So ist das Leben!

Yours,

M

1. Jim Tully, a successful Hollywood journalist and ghost writer, also wrote fiction about the underside of life he had known as a young man among hoboes, circus people, prizefighters, and men in jail. Mencken admired Tully's writing and published several of his stories and articles in the *American Mercury*.

2. Written at Mencken's suggestion, Clendening's book, a general account of physiology for the lay reader, became a best-seller for Knopf. Clendening also contributed articles on medicine to the *Mercury*.

3. As the candidate of the Southern and Western Democrats, backed by the Prohibitionists and the Ku Klux Klan, William Gibbs McAdoo had battled Al Smith for the presidential nomination at the deadlocked 1924 convention. In March 1928, no longer an avowed candidate but seeking to block Smith, McAdoo put forward Senator Thomas J. Walsh of Montana as a candidate. Walsh had earned national recognition for his leading role in the investigation of the Tea Pot Dome and Elk Hills oil-lease scandals. Like Smith, he was a Catholic—a fact his supporters hoped would defuse the charge that they opposed Smith because of his religion.

   Mencken looked upon McAdoo as the heir to William Jennings Bryan in cultivating the "Neanderthal fringe" of the Democratic Party ("McAdoo," *Baltimore Evening Sun* Monday article, 14 Feb. 1927). Of Walsh's candidacy, Mencken had recently written: "No doubt McAdoo would prefer to dispose of Smith with a Ku Klux candidate, . . . but failing a suitable Kluxer he is quite content to try it with a Catholic. If only a cannibal could serve him, he'd probably embrace a cannibal." Though he admired Walsh as a politician of rare personal integrity, Mencken said that the Senator's lack of a sense of humor prevented him from seeing the ridiculousness of accepting not only McAdoo's support but that of the Anti-Saloon League ("Catspaw," Monday article, 9 April 1928).

[TLS]   Baltimore
                                             May 1st [1928]

Dear Gretchen:—

My last chance of hearing any of the concerts at the Library was busted when Jim Tully marched in. He was here Saturday and Sunday, and we had several sessions. He left me the MS. of his new book, "Shanty Irish", and I hope to read it before the end of the week. It is probably capital stuff—the story of his family.

McAdoo be damned. May he wither and pine away. I refuse absolutely to accept his support. He has already ruined poor Tom Walsh.

Your references to living in sin shock me. Such gross wickedness had better not be mentioned. Even thinking of it is foreign to my nature. I am strictly orthodox in that department, and abhor the heresies of Greenwich Village.

Dr. Logan Clendening will be here tomorrow. He has gone on a two-day pretzel diet, with salt herring. But I have enough beer to flood him.

Yours,

M

G.H.: *"Can't recall 'living in sin' or to whom it referred."*

[T L S]   Baltimore
                                               May 5th [1928]

Dear Gretchen:—

Jim Tully has come back for another week-end and I am in a stew. I shall take him to the club again tonight. Last night we had a beer session. He has got into an uproarious row with Upton Sinclair, with threats of suits. The American Mercury may get involved in it. Such are the joys of an editor's life.[1]

The hot weather yesterday restored me to normalcy. I began to sweat like an archbishop, and wrote the whole of The Library for July before 9 P.M. Maybe the Holy Saints are with me again.

Certainly they are not with poor Tom Walsh, for all his piety. His boom came to a dreadful finish.[2]

Beware of Eaton! He has a dreadful way with women.[3]

Yours,

M

1. The quarrel stemmed from Tully's contention that Sinclair had treated him shabbily at the outset of his career. As he told the story, he had taken the manuscript of his first novel to Sinclair, believing that the famous novelist and Socialist would be eager to help an unknown and impoverished novice; after some time, however, Sinclair returned the work

unread. Tully's account was reported in Sara Haardt's portrait of him in the May number of the *Mercury*. Sinclair wrote Mencken, protesting "this slander to me" and producing evidence to the contrary, and later, in a public rebuttal to Tully's charges, noted that he had requested "the Chief Justice of the Supreme Court of the New York Intelligenzia, Henry Louis Mencken," to reverse the verdict ("Jim Tully—A Story of Ingratitude," *Haldeman-Julius Monthly* [Aug. 1928], pp. 7–14).

2. The Walsh candidacy fizzled when he finished a poor third behind Al Smith and James A. Reed in the California primary on May 1.

3. G. D. Eaton, editor of *Plain Talk*. *G.H.:* "Also a worshipper at shrine. . . . A grand guy who came often to drink my beer and 'deplored' the fact I was so 'far gone' on HLM. He died a few years later, of some dread blood-disease. He was years younger than I."

[T L S]   Baltimore
                                           Wednesday [May 9, 1928]

Dear Gretchen:—

As your pastor, I forbid you to commit suicide. It is not only immoral; it is banal. You are quite right about life being a dull round of futilities, but you are wrong in assuming that it would have been any different if you had followed your own free way. I have known, in my time, a great many men who have done precisely what they wanted to do, and made great successes of it. They have ranged from Valentino to H. G. Wells, and from Dreiser to Jake Kilrain.[1] One and all, they were sad men. Only morons are really happy. Only Rotarians believe that the world is charming. But there is something left, and that is curiosity. It is enough to keep us going. As for me, I shall never cut my throat, though I am tempted to do it every time I shave, which is once a day, and twice on days when I attend public banquets and evening weddings. It is my destiny to die upon the public gallows. All the sorcerers say so.

This dreary gale gives me the willies. I am almost homesick for Los Angeles.

                                           Yours,

                                           M

The picture is swell, but you are far more handsomer.

G.H.: *"'Suicide?' It must have been threatened in a joking way be-cause I was caught in a 'bind' of some sort. No such idea ever entered my head."*

1. Kilrain was a heavyweight boxer who lost to John L. Sullivan in seventy-five rounds in the last bare-knuckle championship bout in the United States in 1889. After retiring from the ring in 1896, he lived for several years in Baltimore as an innkeeper and later a rowing coach.

[A P S]   [Bethlehem, Pa.]
                                                             [May 12, 1928]

You should be here, warbling in the B minor mass. The gal who plays the Virgin Mary is nothing compared to you, either as artist or as spectacle.

                                    M

For the first time in four years, Mencken visited Bethlehem for the annual festival of the Bach Choir. In his letter of May 15 (not in-cluded here), Mencken wrote: "The Bach business was only so-so. The chorus, as usual, sang superbly, but the orchestra, also as usual, was terrible. The first trumpet, in fact, dam nigh stopped the mass. His braying sounded like the death agonies of an archbishop."

[T L S]   New York
                                                             May 16th. [1928]

Dear Gretchen:
    Tittmann gave a superb performance.[1] In fact, his singing of the "God Help Us" reduced the whole audience not only to tears, but actually to screams. His voice turned out to be powerful and it threw the trombones out of tune. Moreover, it appeared instantly that he was one of the handsomest men of modern times. You should have been present to share his triumph.

If you actually go to work for the Christian Scientists next year, I shall come to the first service and liberate some mustard gas. The faithful will then have a good chance to prove the efficacy of the Eddian magic.

If you want to be made known to Van Lear Black, let me know. I have long been in charge of his department of social entertainment.

More anon when I get back to the Maryland Free State.

Yours,

M

1. Charles Tittmann, a soloist in the Bethlehem performance of the B minor Mass. *G.H.:* "Co-soloist with me at Unitarian Church at Col[umbia] Rd. & Harvard [St.] N.W. We two were the only singers at that time—no chorus. He made the welkin ring—deep basso & was often so flat I felt I was singing sharp most of time;—strange voice production—his! We were warm pals however."

[TLS]   Baltimore
           May 22nd [1928]

Dear Gretchen:—

Eaton is right. You are simply thunderstruck by my beauty. It is a great nuisance. Whenever I go on the streets women follow me, especially in colored neighborhoods. I am thinking of wearing whiskers.

Eaton has got out an excellent number of his magazine this month. I hope he is comfortable in his job.

I am up to my ears in work, trying to get enough stuff ahead to clear my mind while I am in Kansas City and Texas. Many likely MSS. are coming in, but reading and editing them is a tedious job. I am now writing the August Editorial, and hope to finish one for September before I go. It will have to deal with some neutral and metaphysical subject.

Why not come to Kansas City and sing for the statesmen? They love music.

Yours,

M

[TLS]   Baltimore
                                         Saturday [May 26, 1928]

Dear Gretchen:—
   The beer here has suddenly got bad again. What a world. Early
in the week a superb Dunkles was on tap. It was, in fact, almost
identical with Münchner. But the boozers gobbled it up instanter,
and now the only thing to be had is a poor, gassy, glassy brew with
a drug-store flavor. I begin to despair.
   I hope Eaton doesn't worry about his heart trouble. It will do
him no harm. Men with such things live to be 80. But he ought to
handle booze discreetly. Hall's dithyrambs on Jack Gilbert made me
laugh. Obviously, he is the sort of critic who admires actors. Jack is
really not so bad. But it would be stretching a point to call him
enlightened. He is simply an actor.[1]
   I have been at work in my yard, sawing wood and doing other
heavy work. My back is bent, but I feel pretty good otherwise.
Maybe there is something in exercise after all.
   I hear that Houston will be dry. Oh wurra, wurra!

                                         Yours,

                                         M

1. *G.H.:* "Leonard Hall was dramatic critic here on the News. What a dyna-
   mo! . . . He had me to his enormous apt. many times for musical evenings where I entertained his guests, etc. He really *loved* my voice."
      Hall's "In New York," in the *Washington Daily News,* regularly com-
   mented on Broadway and Hollywood. In his May 23 column, defending
   John Gilbert against a hostile portrait of him by Jim Tully in *Vanity Fair,*
   Hall claimed, "I never knew an actor who had fewer illusions about his
   work. Jack admits, and it is not a pose, that there is a terrific amount of
   tosh about the movies" (p. 15).

[TLS]   Baltimore
                                         June 1st [1928]

Dear Gretchen:—
   Nevertheless, I have warned you.[1] They all say that they are safe,
but then comes the fatal day. I could tell you tales that would make
you bust into sobs.

Pearl is giving a Maryland Free State dinner on Sunday night.[2]
It will be a gaudy affair, but I must hold in my gullet in order to be
alive on Monday morning. For at 9.55 I must depart for the great
city of New York, and there tackle a pile of accumulated work. I'll
clear it off by Thursday. Then for the open spaces.

I look for bloodshed at Houston. The Pope, as you may know,
has landed 5000 Jesuits at Galveston, and they are now in hiding in
the swamps. When they emerge every Christian man in the place
will fall upon them. I expect Tom Heflin to be nominated.[3]

My address at Kansas City will be the [Muehlebach] Hotel. At
Houston I'll be at the Rice Hotel. Both, I hear, are very high-
toned.

Your lovely paw is kissed.

Yours,

Lafcadio[4]

1. On May 29, after Hood had reported that she was spending the weekend
   on a houseboat on the lower Potomac, Mencken had written her: "I warn
   you with all solemnity against booze parties at river shores. They have an
   evil name. Many a poor working girl has come home from one of them
   cursing God. Take your Bible along."

2. Raymond Pearl, noted biometrician at the Johns Hopkins University, became Mencken's close friend and a fellow member of the Saturday Night
   Club and the Maryland Free State Association after Mencken approached him in 1923 to write scientific articles for the *Mercury*.

3. Senator James Thomas Heflin, an Alabama Democrat and a virulent anti-
   Catholic, fiercely opposed Al Smith's candidacy and bolted the Party after
   Smith won the presidential nomination.

4. Why Mencken chose this pseudonym is unclear. In light of his fanciful
   predictions about the Pope and the "bloodshed at Houston," however,
   he may have had in mind the character of this name in André Gide's *Les
   Caves du Vatican*. Alfred Knopf was just about to reissue Dorothy Bussy's
   English translation of Gide's novel, under the title *Lafcadio's Adventures*.
   (Knopf had originally published it in 1925 as *The Vatican Swindle*.) The
   action of Gide's novel, based upon an actual hoax perpetrated by a group
   of swindlers in 1892, revolves around a false rumor that Freemasons have
   imprisoned the Pope in the Vatican cellars and set up an imposter in the
   Holy See.

[A L S]   Hotel Muehlebach
                                               Kansas City, Mo.
                                               [June 11, 1928]

Dear Gretchen:

   This is the usual dull obscenity—roars all day and yells all night.
It is, in fact, even more than usually low-down.[1] I begin to despair
of the Republic. If I must be nominated in 1932 by such vermin I'll
be almost tempted to decline.
   The town is flowing with liquor, but I have kept sober, and shall
keep so until the end. Art first! No one will ever say that I
neglected my chosen art for the low pleasures of the flesh.
   The professor is here, but I have not yet seen him.[2]

                              Yours,

                              M

1. Mencken's initial dispatch to the *Evening Sun* on June 11 predicted "the
   low-downdest Republican National Convention ever heard of" (p. 1);
   with an air of self-fulfilling prophecy, his final dispatch on June 16 was
   headed "This, Says Mencken, Was the 'Most Low-Down' Convention
   Ever Held" (p. 1).
2. Longworth. According to Hood, Mencken awarded him this title after a
   discussion between the two men about bawdy houses. Some years later,
   referring to his youthful adventures in such haunts, Mencken wrote: "I
   was one of the most eminent piano players of that era—in fact, I had only
   one real rival in the whole United States, and that was Nick Longworth.
   He was the doyen of all the Cincinnati professors. We used to compare
   notes in his later years" (letter to Channing Pollock, 13 July 1942, in Forgue,
   Letters, p. 466).

[A L S]   Hotel Muehlebach
                                               Kansas City, Mo.
                                               [June 13, 1928]

Dear Gretchen:

   I was offered second place on the ticket with Al today, and
declined it instantly. First place in 1932, or bust! The Hoover men

have won here, but probably only at the cost of a licking in November. But Al will be slain by bad booze before 1932

I met Mrs. Longworth yesterday, but the professor is not here.[1] The show is only so-so. Vare is now boss of the U. S., and Hoover is to make him Secretary of State.[2] I hear that a coon is to be Secretary of Labor.[3]

Ah, that thou wert here! Old Schumann-Heink sang "The Star Spangled Banner" like a boozy Elk.

Yours,

M

1. With Hoover's nomination likely, Longworth had chosen to go home to Cincinnati instead of to the convention; Alice Roosevelt Longworth, however, was conspicuously present.
2. William Vare, long-time Republican political boss of Philadelphia, was elected to the U.S. Senate in 1926, but was barred from taking his seat after an investigation into his campaign expenditures. On the eve of the Kansas City convention, Vare outmaneuvered Andrew Mellon, his arch-rival in the uncommitted Pennsylvania delegation, by announcing he supported Hoover. His move helped deliver the delegation and effectively sealed Hoover's nomination. As Mencken reported it for the *Evening Sun* on June 12, "the Vare-Mellon episode last night brought the business down to the ultimate nadir of burlesque. For weeks the country had been waiting for word from old Andy. . . . And then the Hon. Mr. Vare, thrown out of the Senate as too foul a bird even for association with Republican Senators, stole the old boy's show away from him" (p. 1).
3. Mencken's tongue-in-cheek predictions about Cabinet appointments reflect his view that Hoover had courted the worst factions of the Republican Party, including the Vare gang and the Southern black party regulars whose political behavior Mencken considered a discredit to the race.

[A P S]   [Kansas City, Mo.]
                           [June 15, 1928]

A swell hotel. The arrow shows the window I spit out of.[1] Despite the filth of politics I remain uncontaminated. The Professor is *not*

here. I suspect the worst. I must read that article about little
Elizabeth Ann.[2] If it comes to a showdown I'll confess.

M

1. The front of the postcard pictures the Hotel Muehlebach.
2. The name is that of the daughter of Nan Britton and President Harding.

[TLS]
Rice Hotel
Houston, Texas
June 25th [1928]

Dear Gretchen:—
   The weather here goes beyond anything ever heard of in the
world. The temperature on the street must be 125, and in the hall it
will run beyond 150. We'll all be pasteurized. But I don't mind it.
The Arkansas coryza has passed, I have found an excellent beer-
house, and God still reigns.[1] I look for a bawdy show in the
convention, which starts tomorrow. There is talk of harmony, but
the Democrats always manage to fight.[2]
   Ritchie thinks he will be the candidate in 1932. I shall not
disillusion him—yet.[3]

Yours,

M

1. Mencken had driven from Kansas City, down through the Ozarks, and on
   to Houston with his colleagues Henry Hyde and Paul Patterson, and his
   hay fever had flared up.
2. Savoring the drama of a convention battle, Mencken anticipated that the
   last-ditch efforts of the "dry" forces to defeat Al Smith would produce a
   donnybrook. The Houston proceedings subsequently disappointed him:
   "the ideal [the Democrats] strive for appears to be a gathering as idiotic
   and innocuous as the late Republican parliament at Kansas City" (*Baltimore Evening Sun,* 27 June 1928, p. 1).
3. Mencken actually felt that the Maryland governor's withdrawal from the
   1928 race had enlarged his influence in Democratic circles and that, should

Smith lose the election, Ritchie had bright prospects for 1932 as "a Protestant hero who can both satisfy the witchburners and soothe the emerging wets" (*Baltimore Evening Sun,* 26 June 1928, p. 1).

[TLS]
          [Houston, Texas]
          Friday [June 29, 1928]

Dear Gretchen:—

The show is over, and righteousness has triumphed. The Al Smith telegram embodies almost word for word the noble doctrine hatched in the Evening Sun office. Ritchie brought it here.[1] I begin to look toward 1932 with serenity.[2] God is on the job.

I am damn nigh all in, what with the noise, the heat and the endless stream of drunken visitors. The hotel is roaring now. I hope to clear out tonight, spend tomorrow in New Orleans, and get back to Baltimore Monday. I have a tale to tell when we meet. It must be soon. That South river place sounds lovely.

As ever,

M

1. Smith's telegram to the convention, accepting the nomination, called for fundamental changes in the Prohibition laws, proposing that the question should be left to state, not federal, jurisdiction. In his last *Evening Sun* dispatch from Houston on June 30, Mencken applauded Smith's declaration for lifting "the whole campaign to a high level of frankness and honesty" after the Democratic platform had straddled the issue; he went on to claim—with his Baltimore chauvinism showing—that Governor Ritchie's states' rights views "now become official Democratic doctrine and the Maryland Free State makes what will probably be a lasting contribution to American political theory" (p. 1).

2. Hood put with Mencken's letters from the conventions a clipping of Frank Sullivan's "Out of a Clear Sky" from the *New York World* of June 21. Sullivan quotes a letter Hood sent him in response to his humorous political commentary attributed to his Aunt Sarah Gallup. "Tell your old Aunt Sarah Gallup to wake up," Hood wrote. "Didn't she conclude her last letter from Kansas City by saying that the next would be devoted to a discussion of the Presidential nominee for 1932? Discussion! Man, there'll be no discussion. It's all fixed. Mencken will be our next President on the Democratic ticket. Tell Aunt Sarah to vote for him." (Clipping in Mencken/Hood Collection.)

[T L S]   Baltimore
                                                    July 3rd [1928]

Dear Gretchen:—

That dream, I suspect, was due to intemperance, a great evil in
these times. The Texan had no desire to assasinate me, though he
flourished his gun in a way to alarm an Easterner. He simply
wanted to show me a good time. When he found out that there
were bullets in the gun he was genuinely astonished. The drunken
owner of it had fooled him.[1]

If you go over to Ritchie, I shall withdraw from the campaign.
His chances seem superficially to be very good in 1928,[2] but the
powers of the air are against him.

I got home with neuralgia, chiggers and a far-away feeling. Three
consecutive nights on sleepers dam nigh finished me—after that
horrible week in Houston. But I begin to feel pretty good today.

I hope you let me come to Washington some time very soon and
have a look at you. I am going to New York on Sunday to clear up
my office, but I'll be back by the end of the week.

The mail accumulated here reached to the ceiling.

                                                    Yours,

                                                    M

1. An exuberant Texan burst into Mencken's hotel room in Houston on a
   lark, asked him if he was being treated right, and then drew a six-shooter
   and fired five shots out the window, creating a small panic in the street
   below and a hotel across the street. Mencken's account of the incident in
   his dispatch to the *Evening Sun* on June 27 evidently prompted the dream
   which Hood related to him.
2. Mencken means 1932.

[T L S]   New York [Baltimore]
                                                July 7th [1928]

Dear Gretchen:—

I am by no means easy in mind about Schmidt. If the election
were tomorrow he would probably beat Hoover, but I have a fear

that he will collapse during the campaign. The New York World is bawling for a refined fight. That is nonsense. The only way to beat Hoover is by killer tactics. I only hope Jim Reed cuts loose against him in the Middle West.

I refuse to let you see Ritchie. The moment you clapped eyes on him you would desert me. He is the handsomest devil ever seen in Christendom. Jack Gilbert is miles behind him. All the gals at Houston curled up when they saw him. Some fainted away.

I have got through my accumulated mail at last, and shall go to New York tomorrow to clean up the office. What a life! I dictated 150 letters in two mornings, and read 40 MSS., all of them bad.

Yours,

M

[TLS]   Baltimore
                                                  July 17th [1928]

Dear Gretchen:—

I protest formally against this weather. It has gone beyond reason. Last night it was roaring hot on my sleeping-porch and I got up and read Holy Writ for an hour. It turns out to be full of lewd and lascivious stuff. I do not recommend it.

I fear that the murder of Obregon will hurt Al. The Ku Kluxers will say that the Catholics did it. Heflin is already charging that they butchered the aviator, Carranza. I only wish they would really cut loose.[1]

My electric fan is red-hot, and still I fume. Maybe the end of the world is at hand.

Yours,

M

1. On July 17, General Alvaro Obregon, the President-elect of Mexico, was assassinated. There were suspicions that the hostility of the Mexican government toward the Catholic Church provoked the killing, despite official denials on both sides, and the assassin later claimed his motive had been to free the Church in Mexico.

Emilio Carranza, a Mexican aviator whose flight from Mexico City to Washington, D.C. in June had made him an instant celebrity, was killed when his plane crashed on his return flight on July 13. Despite the absence of any evidence that Carranza's death was other than accidental, Senator Heflin told the press it was the result of foul play.

[TLS]   Baltimore
                                         July 22nd [July 21, 1928]

Dear Gretchen:—

I surely hope your mother is better and that an operation won't be needed. What a horrible world it is! Every mail brings me news of more illness. I begin to be glad that senility is upon me. A few more years, and then the grand escape from the quacks.

I haven't had on any clothes for a week. If we met thus, it would undoubtedly cause some gossip. But last night the temperature dropped below eighty, and so I had a long sleep. I am still sleepy today. It will take a week to recover.

Broun is going insane. I shall write to him confidentially, telling him that the next White House hostess, after La Schmidt, is already nominated.[1]

Yours,

M

1. Now writing for the *New York Telegram,* Heywood Broun had proposed in his column on July 14 that, instead of relying on the President's choice of a wife for First Lady, the country should have a permanent, nonpartisan White House hostess. He nominated Texas Guinan, the much-publicized New York nightclub hostess of the Prohibition era, as the perfect candidate for the job. "La Schmidt" refers to Mrs. Al Smith.

[TLS]   Baltimore
                                         July 26th [1928]

Dear Gretchen:—

But would connubial bliss be wise? I have some doubts about it. Wouldn't it be better to go down into history as the only Virgin

President ever heard of. I hate to think of those sacred precincts given over to carnal recreations. Give this thought your prayers.

I hope you find a good house. There must be plenty of them. The builders have been overbuilding for five years. Baltimore is full of empty dwellings. Is your mother better? I surely hope so. Please give her my devotion.

Hay fever is not due until August 25th. This year I shall do nothing whatever about it. It is always over by September 12th.

And now more heat! I begin to suspect that the Second Coming may be on us.

> Yours,
>
> M

[TLS]   Baltimore
                                                 August 2nd [1928]

Dear Gretchen:—

I have just got in from New York, to plunge into another infernal spell of heat. Can it be that the Second Coming is really at hand? I begin to give the matter serious thought. All the signs are here save one, and that may come at any minute.

New York is in a low state of mind. The word has gone out that electing Al will be impossible. But wait until the campaign really gets under way! The kikes will regain their courage.

The marriage question, like all other basic human questions, is completely insoluble. It's hell if you do and it's hell if you don't. I begin to suspect that, in the long run, a compromise will be reached by making divorce very easy. That will ameliorate the horror a bit, but it won't dispose of it. I could discourse on this theme at length, but refrain on a/c of the heat.

The Mercury somehow muddles through. I thought it would blow up long ago, but the annual subscribers are still increasing steadily, and it will show a profit this year. God Knows Best.

> Yours,
>
> M

[T L S]
Baltimore
August 7th [1928]

Dear Gretchen:—

I took the afternoon off and dug a hole in the backyard, three feet deep. From it is to rise one of the pillars of a pergola, God giving His sanction. The ground turned out to be so hard that I had to use a hatchet on it. When I finished I looked like a drowned man, and it took twenty minutes under the shower to restore me to normalcy. I must do three more. Then for the bricklaying! It is a refined and difficult art.

What you say of holy matrimony is all sound enough, but what about the case of a man who has taken a vow of celibacy as a sacrifice to his country? Answer me that if you can.

I suppose poor Al is doomed, but he will at least make a tremendous fight. The campaign is still young. Let us be patient and trust in the saints. The Pope prays for him personally every morning. I think the vulgarities of his wife have been greatly exaggerated. She probably reads The American Mercury.

I wish this infernal weather would let up. It has got me half dead.

Yours,

M

[T L S]
Baltimore
August 23rd [1928]

Dear Gretchen:—

It is capital news that your mother is already well enough to come home. Will you please give her my devotion? A dreadful ordeal for both of you, but you have courage, and it brings its reward. I hope she has heard the last of the trouble.

Hay fever is tickling me, and I feel low in mind. I must go to New York within the next week, and I dread the train trip. But a patriot must be willing to sacrifice anything for his country. Look at Coolidge.

The Telegram stuff is bilge.[1] I never answer such things. My spirit is a lofty one. Al will carry every State save Utah, Vermont and Oregon.

Yours,

M

1. Interviewed by the *New York Telegram*, Mencken voiced his fondness for Smith and his familiar gibes against Hoover, but, alluding to his ingrained vision of American politics as a comic spectacle, he noted characteristically that, even if Hoover were elected, "I have a talent for discovering excuses for rejoicing in such bladders" (11 Aug. 1928, pp. 3ff).

The piece aroused controversy in the newspaper the following week. In a parallel interview, Bruce Barton, the advertising executive and author of *The Man Nobody Knows*, dismissed Smith as a candidate and Mencken as his spokesman. "It will be very discouraging to Al to know that Mencken is for him because, of course, Mencken and his boys are always wrong and always licked. They are the sad voices crying in the wilderness, and singing 'Sweet Adeline' in the speakeasies" (17 Aug. 1928, pp. 3ff).

The next day Heywood Broun, taking the side of his fellow newspaperman, challenged Barton's claim that Mencken had an unfortunate influence on the young: "The example Mencken sets to the youngsters of America is one of honesty, courage, and complete candor" (18 Aug. 1928, p. 7).

Still another writer for the *Telegram*, Heyward Kendall, viewing the presidential campaign as a contest between "the ideals of the old Americanism against the new spirit of our cosmopolitan cities," identified Mencken with the latter and, among a torrent of other epithets, laughably mislabled him "dean of the Greenwich Village streptococci" that were poisoning American youth (20 Aug. 1928, p. 3).

[TLS]   Baltimore
                                                   August 31st [1928]

Dear Gretchen:—

You face an immensely difficult problem. I stayed here in Baltimore because my mother was here, and my leaving would have broken up the house. There were plenty of chances to go to New York and even to Europe, but I let them go. Whether I was right or wrong I don't know. I might have done better and been happier in New York, but then again I might have come to grief. I incline to think that you'd be lonely in San Francisco, and probably long for Washington. It is hard to pull up roots. But if you are really bent on leaving Washington it seems to me that your mother ought to yield. Couldn't she look after herself? It is excellent news that she is so much better. Please remember me to her.

I had dinner with Lewis and his wife in New York last Tuesday. She seems very nice. She is as far from No. 1 as you could imagine. No. 1 was very affected; No. 2 is natural and charming. She has rosy cheeks, and is wide enough to look solid and substantial. I liked her very much. Red seems happy and in a good mood for work. He is quieter than he used to be.[1]

Damn the coons! They will have me next. I incline to hold out, and even to invite them to dinner.

Broun fought a gent who had called Dorothy Parker a tart. Apparently the fellow meant no harm. Broun now has two black eyes.[2]

Hay fever has flooded me.

Yours,

M

1. Sinclair Lewis and his new bride, Dorothy Thompson, a foreign correspondent and writer on European political affairs. *G.H.:* "HLM became very much attached to her, & wondered, at the time, how long it would last. He told me of how Lewis' drunken speeches, etc. *bored* his first wife & drove his friends crazy."

2. The purported incident, according to one of Broun's biographers, occurred under different circumstances. A socialite friend of Broun's, a former All-American football player, had chastised another man for insulting his woman companion. Dorothy Parker told him he should pick on someone his own size and nominated Broun, who challenged his friend to a fight. Broun alluded obliquely to the incident in his column for August 20: "It was not a door in some dark room, nor did I slip and fall. Like Dempsey, I forgot to duck" (*New York Telegram*, p. 9; see also Dale Kramer, *Heywood Broun* [New York: A. A. Wyn, 1949], pp. 150–51).

[ALS]   Baltimore
                                         [September 4, 1928]

Dear Gretchen:

The plain fact, I suppose, is that all the really capital human problems are insoluble. Certainly I have never been able to solve any of mine. Staying here, I have missed a lot, including some of the things I wanted most of all. You forget the dreadful drudgery I have gone through for many years. All of my best books remain to be written, and will probably never be written. And I'll certainly never do that string quartette.

So let us console each other! I think you'd be unhappy away from your [?] mother. It is not only your promise to your father: it is something more. You couldn't get rid of it.

Hay-fever is toying with me and I feel like hell. But it will pass. All things pass.

Yours,

M

[TLS]   Baltimore
                                         Saturday
                                         [September 8, 1928]

Dear Gretchen:—

I incline to think that you are right. It seems dreadful that you should waste yourself in Washington. Certainly your mother will see it soon or late. I simply can't imagine her holding out. After all, she can live alone. Suppose your marriage had held out: she'd be alone now. New York I hate, but I think it would be the place for you. There is more music in it than in all the rest of the United States put together.

Hay fever is rather light, and my wrist seems to be getting better. I am giving a beer party tonight, and trust that God will not bust it up. But His will, not ours, be done!

Yours,

M

[TLS]   Baltimore
                                         Friday [October 5, 1928]

Dear Gretchen:—

I hope the flu is mild and almost over   There seems to be an epidemic. Don't let the quacks dose you with drugs. The only cure is prayer.

I am off for New York to join Al. Just when he is to start out nobody seems to know. I hear Monday and I hear Tuesday. In any case your elderly slave will be waiting at the station. I am as eager to see him in action as I was to see the German Army.[1]

The latest news is that he will carry Pennsylvania by 950,000. It seems almost too good to be true.

Yours,

M

1. Mencken covered Al Smith's whistle stop campaign tour through the South and Midwest from October 11 to 21.

[TLS]   Baltimore
                                             Wednesday
                                             [October 24, 1928]

Dear Gretchen:—

My flu seems to be abating, but I am still feeble and work is almost impossible. However, I hope to get out tomorrow. It is good news that you are getting better yourself. My mail is full of tales of death and disaster. Frances Newman died in New York yesterday, and Sara Haardt is in hospital here, following what seems to have been very formidable surgery. I went to a Sun meeting Sunday night, just after getting in. Four of the men present were sick, and one could scarcely stand. No doubt there is a lesson in all this.

Al will be slaughtered. But what a man!

Yours,

M

G.H.: *"This is only time he ever mentioned Sara Haardt. . . . He never spoke of her in any of our conversations. It was all most mysterious— so unlike him not to give me any hint of what lay ahead. Perhaps marriage was not in his mind when he wrote this."*

[T L S]   Baltimore
November 1st [1928]

Dear Gretchen:—

That hookworm infection, or whatever it was, got into my sinuses—and I needn't tell you any more. I have been feeling like a man of 150. But my head has now stopped buzzing and the pains in my legs are passing, and so I hope to come back to normalcy. I dragged myself to the Al meeting on Monday, a foolish thing to do, for I was floored the next day. Were you really there? Why didn't you set up a whoop? I was the nearest man to Al, in the very front row—of the press-stand. I wrote a piece about the meeting, but I was too sick to make it worth reading.[1]

I surely hope that both you and your mother are now well. Every mail brings in news of more sickness. I doubt that Frances killed herself. It was probably pneumonia that took her off.[2]

More when I am back in the Tunney class.[3]

Yours,

M

1. Al Smith opened the final week of his campaign with a speech in Baltimore on October 29, and Mencken's account of it in the *Evening Sun* the next day was much livelier than his comment here suggests. Disappointed by the formal and sober style of Smith's previous addresses, Mencken was delighted that in Baltimore the candidate came out from behind "the lofty, mysterious phrases of the political economist and statistical mortician," and "sailed into all the gods of Moronia in the fashion of a longshoreman cleaning out a saloon. First the Anti-Saloon League was stretched in the sawdust, and then the political parsons, and then the Klan. . . . It was an old-time meeting and it was a grand success" (p. 1).

2. The death of Atlanta novelist Frances Newman was ascribed to natural causes, but an autopsy indicated she had taken an overdose of a sedative.

3. Gene Tunney had recently retired as undefeated heavyweight champion.

[TLS]   New York
                                           November 8th. [1928]

Dear Gretchen:
   I am sorry, indeed, to hear that your mother has had to go back
to hospital. I surely hope that the leeches will now cure her at last.
Will you please give her my best regards?
   I am still rather wobbly, but I am able to work and so feel pretty
good. As usual, I am surrounded by death and disaster. One of my
oldest friends has gone to hospital in Baltimore today for a very
serious operation.
   Yesterday's debacle didn't surprise me. As you know, I came
home from the Smith tour convinced that Al was licked beyond
hope of saving. The plain fact is that the majority of Americans are
Ku Kluxers, and that it is useless to try to beat them by the ballot.
Four years of superb sport looms ahead. Hoover will go into the
White House with the Ku Klux on one shoulder, and the fusileers
on the other. Even if he were honest, he would face a hopeless
situation. I predict that his administration will be one of
continuous scandals and disasters.

                         Yours,

                         M

[TLS]   Baltimore
                                           December 8th [1928]

Dear Gretchen:—
   Nevertheless, you should remember that Mr. Hoover is now
President-elect of the United States. Whatever may be your
opinion of him as a man, you should give him your loyal respect as
Chief Executive of the nation. Let this thought have your earnest
prayers. From this moment forth, any word against him is simply
an encouragement to Liberals, Bolsheviki, Papists, etc. Anon I shall
print an article calling upon all Schmidt men to support him
heartily.

Tell the Professor that I stand in waiting. I'd like very much to see his lady again, but I fear he won't bring her. As for the string quartette, I have shelved it on the advice of counsel. It was growing too noisy. They'd have busted their E-strings.

I am off for New York again—three trips in three weeks. And work is piled up here mountain high. I'll never get any rest until I reach the crematory.

> Yours,
>
> M

[T L S]   Baltimore
                                           Wednesday
                                           [December 19, 1928]

Dear Gretchen:—

Tell La Guardia I'll go on the stump for him if he runs.[1] But he must come out as a 100% wet, and admit publicly that Hoover is an oyster. If he wins I'll make him Secretary of War in 1932.

I am in the hands of my Augenarzt,[2] and making heavy weather of it. My new reading-glasses hurt my eyes, and the professor says that my Chicago infection incommoded the muscles. It sounds very scientific. Thank God, I now have an excuse to increase my saloon hours from 2 to 6 a day. The beer continues very fair, with a rich, clinging foam. Hoover will have a hard time cutting it off. Two more breweries started here last week. The head of one is a prominent Lutheran layman.

It appalls me to hear that the Professor is yielding to his baser appetites. Tell him to remember his high responsibilities. If he ever gives that party I shall whisper to him.[3]

> Yours,
>
> M

1. La Guardia was planning to enter the 1929 New York City mayoralty race. After he lost the election to incumbent Jimmy Walker by almost 500,000 votes, Mencken wrote Hood on November 6, 1929: "La Guardia probably knew what he was about. His defeat was inevitable, but I believe he has improved his position in New York, at least with the Italians. Later on he will show it." Mencken's hunch proved true when La Guardia won the office in 1933.

2. Eye doctor.

3. *G.H.:* "'If he ever gives that party' was a hint of how HLM regarded Longworth. He admired Alice. No, Longworth never gave that party!'"

[T L S]   Baltimore
Heilige Nacht
[December 24, 1928]

Mon chairy Gretchiènne:—
    Au moment des fêtes nous desirons vous dire combien nous apprécions nos cordiales relations et vous adressons nos meilleurs voeux de Noël, et de Nouvel An. Mille Remerciements pour vos bons souhaits. Voeux réciproqués de tout coeur. Joyeux Noël et Bonne Année. Tous nos meilleurs souhaits. Je voudrais être auprès de vous et vous souhaiter de vive vox un Joyeaux Noël et une Heureuse Année.

Hochachtungsvoll![1]

M

    G.H.: "'At the moment of the holiday we wish to tell you how much we appreciate our cordial relations & send our best wishes for Xmas & New Year. A thousand thanks for your good wishes. They are [reciprocated] with all my heart. Merry Xmas & Happy New Year. All our best wishes. I would like to be close to you & salute (toast) you with loud voice "A Merry Xmas & Happy New Year."''"

1. Yours faithfully.

[T L S]   Baltimore
January 5th [1929]

Dear Gretchen:—
    Don't be optimistic. 1929 will be worse than 1928. Every year is worse than all that have gone before. So speaks Zarathustra. I am an old man, and have wisdom.

That French word wasn't an error. It expressed a profound Freudian wish. But such ideas are probably merely fanciful at my age.[1] I can write French beautifully. In fact, I often think of abandoning English for it. English is so gauche.

If you come to Baltimore and don't let me see you I shall get out some sort of writ against you.

Yours,

M

1. Mencken is evidently punning on his use of "chairy" in the salutation in his letter of December 24, 1928.

[T L S]   Baltimore
                                           Saturday [January 12, 1929]

Dear Gretchen:—

What is this intrigue you are carrying on with Villard?[1] I warn you that he is a Red, and in receipt of Moscow Gold. But who am I to throw stones? Tell him I promise to make him Secretary of State, and to have Borah boiled in oil.[2] Kellogg we needn't bother about.[3] He will be in the arms of Jesus long before 1932.

I have scrapped the big book that I was planning to write, and shall first do a shorter one.[4] I hope to get to work on it next week. It will be far easier to write than the big one, and probably much better. It will be devoted mainly to examining the character and career of God. You are put down for an absolutely free copy, elegantly autographed.

You are not the reincarnation of George Sand! I refuse to let anyone say it. In the last life you were Queen Elizabeth.

How is your mother? I surely hope she is much better. As for me, I continue to move from malaise to malaise.

Yours,

M

1. Oswald Garrison Villard, outspoken editor of the *Nation*. G.H.: "I met him at a public speaking affair—enjoyed a 'lively' conversation with him."

2. Senator William E. Borah, Republican from Idaho.

3. Frank Billings Kellogg, Secretary of State under Coolidge.

4. The writing of *Treatise on the Gods* occupied Mencken until November.

[TLS]   Baltimore
                                          January 31st [1929]

Dear Gretchen:—

A war with England? Do you want to see me laugh myself to death? It would be the gaudiest show ever heard of in the world. My one fear is that I'll be summoned to the right hand of God just before it begins. Try to imagine the bawling on both sides! The whole thing would be incomparable, unbelieveable, colossal.[1]

I was in Union Hill, N.J., the night of Gieseking's performance.[2] Knopf represented me at the ringside. He reported that the sounds were very sweet. In Union Hill I heard no music, but the malt liquor was very fair. One can't have everything.

I know of no gal who has lately lost her husband. It seems highly unlikely: my spies always report such things. Nor do I recall any fair one who was a Christian Scientist. It ought to be interesting. I shall send out scouts.[3]

The quacks entertain themselves with my sinuses, and my head feels like a beer barrel. Science is really marvellous. I hope to be well in 10 or 12 years. Did you read Cal's article about the discomforts of life in the White House?[4] I[t] gave me pause. But if my country calls, there I shall be. Everything for the Flag!

                                                  Yours,

                                                    M

1. There was a flurry of debate in the press over the possibility of such a war, growing out of the British and American naval rivalry. In his Monday article for February 18, 1929, Mencken dismissed "this pother," arguing that the English would never enter a war they knew they would lose and concluding that their bellicose noises were designed to blunt the American challenge to their control of the seas—an aim abetted by "the pacifists and the Anglomaniacs" in this country.

2. Pianist Walter Gieseking played at Carnegie Hall on January 23.

3. The lady in question is most likely Marion Bloom. Her attraction to
   Christian Science had contributed to her break with Mencken. At this
   time she had divorced her husband and returned from abroad, and she
   and Mencken wrote one another occasionally.

4. In an article published in the fiftieth anniversary issue of the *St. Louis Post-
   Dispatch* on December 9, 1928, Coolidge wrote of the demands that life in
   the White House placed on the physical well-being of the President, but
   affirmed that "a man of ordinary strength can carry them" if he rigorously
   restricts himself to his constitutional and legal duties and resists all the
   other public commitments that are pressed upon him "with the inference
   that unless he responds civilization will break down and the sole responsibility will be on him" (quoted in full in *New York Times*, 10 Dec. 1928,
   pp. 1–2).
   Mencken humorously applauded the article as a masterpiece of folk art
   which, both in its style and its substance, revealed "the real Calvin
   Coolidge" ("Cal as Literatus," *Baltimore Evening Sun* Monday article, 24
   Dec. 1928). His upcoming March editorial for the *American Mercury* commented on the "intimate revelations" of the hardships of presidential life.
   To Coolidge's claim that he was the healthiest President the nation had
   ever had, Mencken responded: "Let the historians put it down. The
   chances seem very good that when they come to write the Coolidgiad
   they will have little else to say" (16:279–80).

[TLS]   Baltimore
                                               March 9th [1929]

Dear Gretchen:—
  God has been having some fun with me of late. My head
infection travelled down to the air-pipes and I have been wheezy
and very uncomfortable. The quacks look wise, but do nothing. I
had hoped to witness the inaugural orgies, but at the last minute I
changed my mind, probably wisely, for the rain would have done
me more damage than it did to fat Herbert.
  It is capital news that you are going to the Bach Choir festival.
I'll be there with Knopf, and ready to show you the town kaifs.
Last May they were dry, but I hear that good beer is on tap again.[1]
In any case I shall bring some reliable gin. Let us hold hands while
they sing the great Erdner Treppchen motif in the B minor mass. It
always makes me blubber. Have you got a place to live in

Bethlehem? If you have no reservation you had better make it at once. The town is always jammed. Last year I staid at the Bethlehem Club, but this time Knopf is trying to get a room in the hotel.

Tell the Professor I am waiting.

Yours,

M

1. The previous year Mencken had lamented that he found only a "depressing bilge" instead of the excellent brew he remembered from earlier times, when "Bethlehem was still magnificently beery, and the crowds that came to hear the choir moved in a steady and orderly manner from saloon to saloon, getting into the right mood for Bach" ("Bach at Bethlehem," *Baltimore Evening Sun* Monday article, 21 May 1928).

[T L S]

Baltimore
Friday [May 10, 1929]

Dear Gretchen:—

What became of your plan to go to Bethlehem? Are you really disabled? I surely hope not. Your letter has just come in and I am off in ten minutes. Getting to the fire-ground is a dreadful business. It takes longer than getting to New York. I hope to find good beer this year.

Tell La Guardia to beware. There are eight nicks in my gun handle.

Yours,

M

G.H.: "*The writer who introduced me to La G. told me he said he'd ask me to marry him but for the fact I was 'too far gone' on Mencken & could 'never see him.' I didn't play my cards right.*"

[T L S (postscript handwritten)]   Baltimore
                                     May 19th [1929]

Dear Gretchen:—
  It is too damned bad about your wrist. I surely hope the
chiropractors repair it. I am in their hands myself. My antr[u]m
infection revived at Bethlehem, and I feel like hell. But a few shots
of argerol in the head ought to dispose of it. I am eager to get back
to work on my book, which promises to be a masterpiece. For the
pain I recommend ethyl alcohol. It is better than poppy or
mandragora.
  The Bach Choir performed the B minor mass superbly, but the
Matthew Passion was only so-so. Tittmann did some noble
bawling. The poor tenor, as usual, made a fearful mess of it. I
suspect that Bach hated tenors, as Beethoven did. Like all good
composers, he prferred castrati.
  Perhaps I should not conceal from you further the fact that I am
gradually incliding toward Hoover.* The man has intelligence of a
high order, and is a true Christian. His speech on Law
Enforcement was unanswerable.[1] After all, we must try to cherish
respect for the constituted authorities. If they are flouted, then we
have revolution and chaos.

                              Yours,

                              M

*I put him above Coolidge and almost on a level with Harding and
Kellogg.

1. Speaking on April 22 at an Associated Press luncheon in New York,
   Hoover warned that lawlessness threatened "a subsidence of our founda-
   tions" and called for a reawakening of the national consciousness to up-
   hold the sanctity of the law (*New York Times*, 23 April 1929, p. 2). Mencken
   had, in fact, issued a blistering answer in his Monday article of April 29.
   The present disrespect for the law flourished, he charged, not because of a
   moral failure of the American people, but because under Prohibition "the
   law has become synonymous with tyranny and corruption, and its agents
   are the worst criminals at large among us." Mencken declared, as "the

soundest sort of Jeffersonian doctrine," that when the law "is palpably vicious, the good citizen declares himself against it, and tries his best to have it repealed. And when, because of constitutional difficulties, also vicious, he finds that repealing it is impossible, he serves the common weal and common decency by violating it."

[TLS]   Baltimore
                                                   June 21st [1929]

Dear Gretchen:—

What a holiday! But you say nothing about the wines and liquors. How could an elderly man stand weeks on a house-boat without his regular drams? Also, there is the matter of news. How could an old journalist live without Hoover's speeches? All the same it must have been lovely.

I am plugging away at the book, and sweating to death. The temperature in my laboratory has run up to 100, and has seldom gone below 80. But I must be brave, for my Public expects much of me. Ah, this Art! What a sad taskmistress! Sometimes I almost wish that I had staid in the garage business.

You are unjust to Clarence True Wilson. He is an honest man, but has been fooled by God. It happens not infrequently. The notion that our Heavenly Father has no sense of humor is simply boloney. Think of what he has just done to Bishop Cannon![1]

Are you to be in New York this Summer?

                                                   Yours,

                                                   M

1. Wilson, the General Secretary of the Methodist Board of Temperance, Prohibition and Public Morals, and Bishop James Cannon, Jr., were both Methodist clergymen and powerful figures in the Prohibitionist ranks. Bishop Cannon reached his peak of national influence when, as a leader of the anti-Smith faction within the Democratic Party, he was instrumental in helping the Republicans carry several Southern states, including his own Virginia. He was subsequently courted by the Hoover administration as an ally and counselor—a preeminence which prompted Mencken to proclaim him "the first Pope the United States has ever had" ("Doctor Illuminatus et Sublimus," *Baltimore Evening Sun,* 18 March 1929). The

bishop had recently come under fire, however, for playing the stock market. Mencken surveyed his predicament as a moral zealot hoisted on his own petard in several subsequent Monday articles during the summer of 1929.

[T L S]   Baltimore
                                                           July 19th [1929]

Dear Gretchen:—

Don't talk to me of swimming and crabbing! I am afraid of the water, and never go near it. When I was a boy my Uncle Wolfgang, while in his cups, rolled overboard and was never seen again; the incident ruined my youth. What do you do about chiggers? They are all over Anne Arundel county. Also, what of mosquitoes, gnats, bumble-bees, wasps, etc.? Also, what of Methodists and Baptists? Also, what of Prohibition agents? You are trying to kill me!

The book is moving along. It will be larger than I expected, and a damned sight more superber and idealer. In fact, it begins to take on a very high tone. But the higher the tone, the more difficult the labor. I'll be at it for months.

                                                           Yours,

                                                           M

Mencken wrote Hood at Deale, Maryland, where she was vacationing on Chesapeake Bay.

[T L S]   Baltimore
                                                           August 15th [1929]

Dear Gretchen:—

You tempt me with that Willys-Knight, but I stick to my oath: no automobiles save taxicabs, and no trip of more than three miles. The roads are covered with broken glass, twisted steel, and blood. Moreover, bumping along hurts my gluteus maximus. Make it a Pullman and you have me booked. When they kill, it is swiftly, and there are damages for the heirs.

Hay-fever has begun to toy with me. Like Coolidge and Aristotle, I must look for it every Autumn. I don't sneeze much, but my mind gets low. Ah, that thou wert near to comfort me! But you are never on land.

I am on the last lap of the book. It will be, I believe, a swell job. I look for a Harvard LL.D.

Yours,

M

[TLS]   Baltimore
                                                 September 3rd [1929]

Dear Gretchen:—

Hay fever has me by the gills and I feel very low and Christ-like. If it passes by the end of the week I may go down to Charlotte, N.C. for a few days to have a look at the trial of the accursed communists.[1] My agents report that it promises to be a good show. But in any case I'll be in New York by the 17th. Do I have the honor of seeing you at lunch? I surely hope and pray so. Let me hear of it as soon as you find out precisely when you'll be there. I can promise you a very fair bottle of vin.

Essary had nothing to do with those articles. Surely it is no secret that they were written by M—— S——.[2] But don't tell anyone. Seriously, everyone has guessed wrong. The villain is not even suspected. If Hoover knew the truth he would bust.

The book is making slow and sad progress. God is against it.

Yours,

M

1. Mencken did not attend the trial of thirteen labor organizers accused of murdering the police chief of Gastonia, North Carolina, during the textile workers' strike. The trial was halted on September 9, when one juror was declared insane.

2. *G.H.*: "I think M. S. means Mark Sullivan." The Washington columnist for the *New York Tribune* and the author of *Our Times: The United States from 1900–1925*, Sullivan was a close friend of Hoover and was considered the journalistic voice of his administration.

Hood does not identify the articles in question. Possibly, they were two which appeared in the July and August numbers of the *Mercury*, signed simply "a Washington Correspondent." The first was the aforementioned piece on Mabel Walker Willebrandt. The second burlesqued Vice-President Charles W. Curtis as obsessed by the belief that "but for a foul deal of fate he might have been nominated as President, and that even today there stands between him and his consuming ambition only a fat, harried and distraught man" ("Heap Big Chief," 17:401–11). Though unsigned, both articles are very much in the style of Duff Gilfond. If her friend wrote them, Hood probably knew it, but she may have reported to Mencken that Fred Essary, his Washington colleague on the *Sunpapers*, was rumored to be the author, provoking this jesting counter-attribution.

[T L S]   Baltimore
                                       September 12th [1929]

Dear Gretchen:—

I am sorry indeed to hear that your mother is still ill. What a horror it is to get into the hands of the faculty! I hope she gets better quickly, and that you can come to New York after all.

I have had a wretched week, but feel better, and am looking forward to a roaring beer party on Saturday night. If I drink less than five hectoliters the governor of the feast is licensed to give me a swift kick a posteriori.

God help us all!

                                       Yours,

                                       M

Don't move! The coons may be bad, but they are better than whites.

[T L S]   Baltimore
                                       September 30th [1929]

Dear Gretchen:—

I surely hope your mother is much better. Please remember me to her. My own malaises seem to be passing. I threw away all philtres and put my trust in prayer alone. Tell the flutist he is mashuggah. Going off alcohol and meat would cause the gall-stones to block up the bronchii. A better scheme would be to go on a diet of gunpowder and blood.

I see no reason why you shouldn't give some lessons to the Moor. You don't have to do it in class. In fact, no one need know that you are doing it. Certainly he deserves some help. I am instructing my sorcerers to do their stuff for your pupil. Another prize and you will win the gold loving-cup of Marchesi.[1]

I labor hard, but the book still refuses to be finished. God's hand is in this. I wish I could come to the concerts at the Library, but it looks impossible.

Yours,

M

1. Another of Hood's students, Florence Yokum, was competing in the Atwater Kent vocal auditions. Mathilde Graumann Marchesi was an internationally known teacher of voice and founder of the École Marchesi in Paris, where her pupils included Emma Calvé, Mary Garden, and Nellie Melba.

[T L S]   Baltimore
                                         December 14, 1929.

Dear Gretchen:

I gather from your letter that you are now a rich woman. It is swell news indeed, and as soon as I get back from Europe I shall give you a chance to lavish some of your money on a handsome man.

I am sailing the day after Christmas, and shall be gone until the end of February. The first two or three weeks I hope to spend in the saloons of Paris and Munich. After that I am going to London to help cover the naval conference for the *Evening Sun*. Do you want me to send you any picture postcards? If so, what kind do you prefer?

Yours,

M

On Christmas day Mencken sent Hood the following telegram: "English spies have blown up the Columbus. Maybe my sailing will be delayed. I shall bring you a diamond sunburst. The best of luck in Nineteen Thirty." A month later he sent her a valentine from London.

[TLS]
Baltimore
March 26th [1930]

Dear Gretchen:—

You rout me out of my mood of scholarly abstraction. Anon I shall surely give myself the honor of waiting on you. Let the Burgundy stand on the sideboard five days; the Sauterne may be chilled at the last moment. I hear from private sources that you are more beautiful than ever, what with your reducing and an active outdoor life, with plenty of Alpine life. I wish I could say the same for myself. But the plain fact is that I am breaking up. A year of theology grayed me, and bent my back. I begin to look like an early Christian martyr.

Mrs. Bentley gave me the good news that your mother is now quite well. Please remember me to her.

I have a fear that you will find the book somewhat dullish. A certain heavy learning got into it. Most of the reviews are slatings, which is good news, for slatings sell books.[1] Having written no book for three years, I have suffered from anemic royalties. Now they will fatten a bit, which is only one more proof of the mercy of God.

What are you up to? I suspect you of designs on old Charlie Curtis yourself. Don't deny it! He is a handsome man.[2]

Yours,

M

1. Mencken's skeptical stance toward all religious dogma, and especially toward the modern role of Christianity, aroused indignation or derision

particularly among religious-minded reviewers. But the reception of *Treatise on the Gods* was not uniformly hostile; some commentaries praised its knowledgeable and lucid exposition of its case. Within the year, sales exceeded 13,000 copies.

2. In his next letter, dated May 16, Mencken continued: "I still insist that you have felonious plans against poor Curtis. However loudly you protest, I can only believe the reports of my spies. But I don't blame you. He is a handsome fellow, and I hear rumors that in recent years he has accumulated a comfortable fortune. His Indian blood, I hear, seldom boils." Vice-President Curtis had some Kaw and Osage blood, which he made much of in his campaigns for office.

[T L S]   Baltimore
                                          August 7, 1930.

Dear Gretchen:

I'll never believe that you are really an aviator until I see you go up. When is that to be? Say the word, and I'll come over to Washington at once.

I suppose you have heard of my approaching marriage. The bride is a rich woman and promises to treat me tenderly. She is worth at least $7000 in gilt-edge bonds, class A common stocks, unencumbered farm lands and down-town real estate.

By the way, *what is Mrs. Gilfond's address?* I have a telegram from her but don't know how to reply to it.

I also received a wireless from La Guardia.

Yours,

M

G.H.: *"This was the worst shock I ever had—never heard him mention to me Sara Haardt's name. I had to read about it in the papers before I got this. In reply I wrote 'I only ask that I be permitted to sing "You Promised Me" at your wedding. I hope you will be the most militantly happy husband in captivity.' I never got over it."*

[TLS]   New York
                                                August 14th. [1930]

Dear Gretchen:
  My very best thanks. I am writing to La Gilfond at once.
Would you consider an offer of $5000 cash to sing "Die Wacht
am Rhein" at the wedding? The whole service will be in the
Hunnish language. Let me have your prayers.

                                    Sincerely,

                                    HLM

G.H.: *"Don't you love that 'Sincerely'?"*

[TLS]   704 Cathedral St.[1]
                                                Baltimore
                                                June 11, 1935.

My dear Gretchen:
  I am distressed indeed to hear of your mother's illness and all
your troubles. I begin to believe that the celestial Brain Trust is
even worse than the gang of quacks now reigning in Washington.
Certainly I seem to be surrounded by woe and lamentation. My
poor girl had been ill for a long while past, but she was always so
patient and courageous that it never occurred to me that there
could be a fatal termination Thus her sudden death from
meningitis was a colossal shock, and I find myself so played out
that I can't do anything resembling sensible work. I am thinking of
going abroad for a few weeks with my brother, who has been ill
too.[2] Unluckily, we can't stay long, for I am confronted with an
enormous pile of undone work and it must be tackled very soon.
  I hope you let me see you when I get back. It seems a long, long
while since our last meeting.
  Please remember me to your mother.

                                    Yours,

                                    H. L. MENCKEN

1. The address where the Menckens had lived since their marriage.
2. Mencken and his brother August went to England on June 14 and returned July 12.

Mencken's letter was in response to the letter of condolence Hood wrote him on June 10:

> Dear Henry Mencken:
>   May I tell you how sorry I am over your recent bereavement? Any words I write can do little good, but I at least want you to know my deep sympathy is with you. I can only hope your own philosophy will see you through— Heaven knows it holds more soundness & consolation than anything the theologians offer.
>   Well, at least you have had five years of happiness and that is more than some of us get. Life seems to be made up of never getting the things we want and of losing the things we love most. These past five years have been pure hell for me. We managed to keep the roof over our heads, but that's about all. Mother lost virtually all her income and then was worried into a state of permanent illness over that, and the fear that the Ass'd. Press would cut off her miserably inadequate monthly allowance, which they threatened to do. She now spends most of her days in bed,—heart trouble—and is forbidden to exert herself in any way. No going up & down steps—no anything that made up her old life. All of the house work, cooking, furnace—in fact everything, is now up to me & I feel able to qualify as a longshoreman or stevedor. My pleasures are now very simple: a cigarette now & then, a good symphony, a first-rate book, a glass of beer when I'm thirsty;—that's about all!
>   Please be sure my sympathy is with you. Some day, when the tide of your mail is at a low ebb (if ever) won't you please write and tell me about it, if you care to?
>   Sincerely,
>   MISS GRETCHEN HOOD

(Original in Goucher College Library.)

[T L S]   704 Cathedral St.
                                                             Baltimore
                                                             July 30, 1935.

My dear Gretchen:
  It goes without saying that I'd be really delighted to see you.
Don't you ever come to Baltimore? Some time ago some one told
me that you had been at Schellhase's here for dinner.[1] I surely hope
you let me hear of it the next time you make the trip. I'll be in New
York all of next week, but after that I'll be here continuously until
the end of September. I had hoped to get to Washington before
this, but I have been so hard at work on the rewriting of my old
book, "The American Language", that it has been impossible.[2]
  It is good news about your pupils. Where were the sonnets
printed?[3] And why haven't I seen them? If you have any copies in
hand I'll be delighted to read them. My own writing during the
past six months has been done with the left hand. Hereafter I hope
to buckle down to serious work.
  My guess is that Hitler will be bumped off on some near
tomorrow. The Junkers are tiring of him. Some day they'll rise up
and cut his throat. They are rough fellows.

                                                             Yours,

                                                             M

G.H.: *"I went to Balt. very often, to visit others but never called him or
took him up on his invitation—I was too completely 'done in' even after 5
years & never able to forgive him, particularly for the heartless way it was
done. . . . That did it. I was through."*

1. The new Schellhase's, on Howard Street, had become the regular haunt
   of the Saturday Night Club.
2. The extensively expanded and rewritten fourth edition of Mencken's major work appeared in 1936.
3. G.H.: "They were printed in Walter Winchell's columns throughout the
   U.S."

[T L S]   704 Cathedral St.
                                            Baltimore
                                            December 21, 1935.

My dear Gretchen:
    Thanks so much for your card and your good note. I have been
inquiring for you at Schellhase's, but have always got the answer
that you have not been there of late. I surely hope you resume your
pilgrimages very soon, and that you give me a chance to see you. I
was in Washington last week, but only for a few hours, and all of
my time was taken up with newspaper business. I hope you let me
see you the next time I make the trip. That will probably be very
soon.
    Please remember me to your mother. I surely hope that she is
much better than she was the last time I heard from you.

                                            Yours,

                                            HLM

[T L S]   Baltimore
                                            March 12, 1937.

Dear Gretchen:
    It was grand to hear from you again, and I only hope that you
let me see you soon.
    Clarke Beach is doing very well on the Baltimore *Sun*.[1] Some
time ago he was put in charge of a daily column. It has been a
considerable success and he is filling it with good stuff.
    My illness was not serious, but only a nuisance. I got into
hospital at Christmas with a throat infection, and after being
liberated came down with something else. I therefore returned to
the slaughter, and after a small operation was discharged once
more.
    La Guardia seems to me to be an excellent cook, but otherwise a
dreadful jackass. His uproars can have only one effect. Soon or late
they will inevitably stir up an anti-Semitic movement in the United
States. Most Americans are sympathetic to the Jews, but they hate
to be dragged into all of the Jews' quarrels.[2]

My brother and I are keeping bachelor hall in this house. My sister spends most of her time on a little farm in Carroll county, and when she is in town she lives in a flat. We have a good cook, and a cellar that is worth speaking of with respect.[3] I surely hope you drop over to Baltimore sometime soon, and that you let me see you. When I'll be in Washington again God only knows.

Tell Kindler that his speech has so affected me that I have decided to give him $100,000.[4] The check, in fact, is enclosed herewith. Tell him I'll go even further—that is, I hereby agree, in case any of his leading performers are hanged or otherwise disposed of, to come to Washington and take their places.

Yours,

HLM

G.H.: *"I never answered this. Suppose I was God's Greatest Goof not to have picked up the threads, but I felt I couldn't ever believe in him or trust him again. He was too big a person to have hurt me so!"*

1. A family friend of Hood's.
2. Speaking before the women's division of the American Jewish Congress on March 3, Mayor La Guardia said that if he were designing the upcoming World's Fair, he would include a "chamber of horrors" highlighted by a figure of "that brown-shirted fanatic who is now menacing the peace of the world." His remarks provoked a formal protest from the German government. After Secretary of State Cordell Hull formally apologized on behalf of the United States, La Guardia declared that he stood by his condemnation of the Nazi regime. His stand produced heated debate between anti-Fascist and pro-German sympathizers in this country, and brought on a storm of vilification in the government-controlled German press against La Guardia, the American Jewish community, and the American people—an outburst that led, in turn, to an official American protest to the German government on March 11.

The essential incompatibility between La Guardia's outlook and Mencken's surfaced here in the much-changed political climate of the 1930s. Like his reference to Hitler in his letter of July 30, 1935, Mencken's criticism of La Guardia reflects his persistent underestimation of the nature and magnitude of the Nazi madness that had transformed the Germany he so admired.

3. Mencken had moved back to Hollins Street in March 1936 to live with August. Hester Danby, who had worked for him and Sara, kept house for the two brothers.

4. Hans Kindler, founder and conductor of the National Symphony Orchestra.

Index

About the Editor

Peter W. Dowell teaches English and American Studies at Emory University.
He received his B.A. from Princeton University
and his M.A. and Ph.D. from the University of Minnesota.